The

Southern Way

The regular volume for the Southern devotee

Kevin Robertson

Issue 50

www.crecy.co.uk

We just could not find an engine with a 'Southern Way' headboard...? But perhaps this is better as most of us like chocolate! No 34038 at Tyseley (Birmingham) having worked a special from... well certainly the Southern Region. (Does anyone have any information?) Unfortunately no date and please note we have deliberately avoided the puns like, "Was there a bar on the train..?" and "Whisper it quietly but…". *Wilf Stanley/Transport Treasury*

Opposite: In glorious 'Technicolor' and enhanced by the side lighting, No 34019 displays its brilliance at Eastleigh following overhaul, 3 October 1964. According to 'The Book of …' (Irwell Press), this had been a 'Light Intermediate' lasting from 8 August to 1 October. No 34019 would receive two more unclassified repairs, the first in 1965 and the last the following year. She lasted until March 1967, withdrawn from Nine Elms having run just over 700,000 miles in a life of just over 21 years. (Eastleigh's cleaners may have had their moments, but it was a long time since an engine had been prepared to this standard at the shed – except for a special working that is. That said, towards the very end the shedmaster would pay overtime to firemen (and sometimes drivers) who were prepared to come in and clean the worst of the muck of various engines. It was an incentive that worked well, so whilst leaking joints and the odd wheeze (or three) may have been commonplace, at least they were 'cleaner wheezes!') *Peter Gray/Great Western Trust*

© 2020 Crécy Publishing Ltd
and the various contributors

ISBN 9781909328952

First published in 2020 by Noodle Books
an imprint of Crécy Publishing Ltd

New contact details
All editorial submissions to:
The Southern Way (Kevin Robertson)
'Silmaril'
Upper Lambourn
Hungerford
Berkshire RG17 8QR
Tel: 01488 674143
editorial@thesouthernway.co.uk

A CIP record for this book is available from the
British Library

Publisher's note: Every effort has been made to
identify and correctly attribute photographic
credits. Any error that may have occurred is
entirely unintentional.

Printed in the UK by Cambrian Printers Ltd

Noodle Books is an imprint of
Crécy Publishing Limited
1a Ringway Trading Estate
Shadowmoss Road
Manchester M22 5LH

www.crecy.co.uk

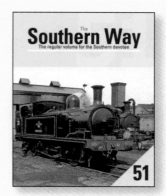

Issue No 51 of THE SOUTHERN WAY
ISBN 9781909328983
available in July 2020 at £14.95
To receive your copy the moment it is
released, order in advance from your usual
supplier, or it can be sent post-free (UK)
direct from the publisher:

Crécy Publishing Ltd (Noodle Books)

1a Ringway Trading Estate, Shadowmoss
Road, Manchester M22 5LH

Tel 0161 499 0024

www.crecy.co.uk
enquiries@crecy.co.uk

Front cover:
Guildford shed plays host to E4 radial tank No 32505 on
15 June 1959. Built at Brighton in 1900 it remained in
LBSCR territory for most of its life having been recorded
at Brighton in 1948, Fratton in 1953 before reaching
Guildford in 1955. Its final depot was Nine Elms from
May 1960 where after a spell on pilot and carriage
shunting duties it was withdrawn in March 1961.
Peter Gray/Great Western Trust

Rear cover:
Almost watched by two youthful spotters, 6 PUL unit
No 3006 entering Brighton complete with its single
Pullman car. This is likely to have been Car 'Anne'.
Graham Smith, courtesy Richard Sissons

Title page:
Mixed liveries at Folkestone with a pair of water tank
cars in tow. *Graham Smith, courtesy Richard Sissons*

Contents

Introduction

I am breaking my supposed self-imposed rule again with this issue; and that is not to refer specifically to any particular piece that follows for fear of appearing to show favouritism. Having of course read the various contributions included I cannot help but be taken aback by the action of our forebears as described by Jeremy Clarke in his piece on the Croydon Tangle. My goodness, here was indeed a tangle of lines; makes me quite exhausted just getting my head around it all. And I have to say that having an atlas open when studying the piece is certainly recommended.

The two items Jeremy includes that to me really stand out are how competition between railway companies (operators in twenty-first century terms) was enacted on the ground. Speaking specifically of Godstone Road (Caterham Junction) and the antagonism exercised on the ground between the staff of the South Eastern and Brighton companies, Jeremy comments, "Among other obstacles the LBSCR refused 'through' booking but then provided little time for tickets to be purchased before the connecting services departed. It would appear that in some instances the booking offices remained defiantly closed and on occasions passengers who had managed to purchase tickets were forcibly detained to prevent their making connections." We then have the total opposite years later when following a necessary timetable and London terminal change, "Herbert Walker wrote personally to every season ticket holder...explaining why this had become necessary." We may not suffer quite the same difficulties today but the current railway operators do sometimes need to look to the past and relearn the same lessons.

This issue also contains the final instalment of the 'Lost Archives of Stephen Townroe'. We have run this for some fifteen editions of SW, nearly four years in total and I am personally very sad we have reached the end. As I may have recounted earlier, the series all came about following an unexpected call from the Townroe family to say that in a box marked 'jig saws' they had come across a number of negative packets....and would I like to see them? The results you will all know by now and we can all be grateful for their recognition that this was indeed something rather special. All I can say, both for myself and on behalf of the readers of 'SW', is a genuine 'thank you'; and should you ever come across any other boxes marked in similar fashion do please get in touch!

As this is a commemorative issue we have also included rather more photo sections than would normally be the case. I do hope you enjoy the results. I will certainly not say 'normal service will be resumed next time' as what indeed is 'normal'? The intention is to continue including items we hope you enjoy as well as a few 'off the wall' pieces from time to time.

Thank you for staying the course, or joining us whenever that has been.

Kevin Robertson

Opposite top: **One for which we need your help. *'Southern Way needs YOU!'* and all that. Simply put, where is it? L1 4-4-0 No 31753 crossing, we would suggest, the Brighton line. So assumption is: ex-SECR train and LAV unit. The only thing we could say with certainty is the road alongside would not be anywhere near as quiet now. Much searching of various books and maps has already taken place but this is one where specific local knowledge is required.**

Bottom: **Clapham Junction carriage sidings, undated but with a proliferation of liveries so likely to be early 1950s without, it appears, a Mk1 to be seen. Two Bulleid sets are possibly identified, Nos 820 and 292, although the former may be noted as having different liveries within, so we are assuming it is indeed still a fixed formation. Set 820 was of three vehicles: semi-open Brake 3rds Nos 4279 and 4280 with seven-compartment composite No 5813 between. Set 292 was of six vehicles: semi-open brake third No 4353, seven-compartment composite No 5742, corridor/restaurant first No 7679, restaurant/kitchen third No 7883, open-saloon third No 1453 and finally another semi-open brake third No 4354 (information from Mike King's *Southern Coaches* of course!). Other vehicles but identified only in general terms are from the Maunsell era as well as bogie utility vans and Pullman cars.**

Fratton shed in November 1949 with T9 No 30287, M7 30045 and an unknown C2/C2X as well as a long defunct carriage body minus wheels in the background. The image is included as a hint as to what is to follow shortly for Mike King has offered to provide some articles on grounded coach bodies – I for one look forward to this immensely. Grounded coach bodies used to be a regular feature of both the landscape as well as here on railway property. In the latter case, perhaps extra storage or messing space or even, as in the case at Eastleigh, used as a canteen. In the former they could become anything from a home to a shed – even stables or a chicken coop. Few survive today and what do have probably been altered beyond all recognition. Fortunately some eagle eyed observers became aware of the existence of some of the survivors and railways like the Bluebell had the presence of mind to save examples which future generations may now enjoy restored to their original purpose as proper 'rolling stock'. Do let us know if you know of any remaining examples (SR rolling stock that is and not former BR covered vans) still serving a purpose 'out to grass' in some field or other; but do please also respect private property.

And speaking of grounded bodies, one to 'wet the appetite', the carriage portion of 'the Bug' grounded since about 1940 and in use at Eastleigh Carriage works. It was subsequently rescued by Reg Curl and for many years served as a waiting shelter on his Durley Light Railway. It has since been moved to private premises in Swanage. Looking inside during the time it was in Hampshire revealed the circular plate at one end which could be rotated so Mr Drummond could pass instructions (should that nay be demands...?) to the engine crew. The ceiling decoration is also recalled as embossed paper/plaster in rectangular and longitudinal pattern.

The Lost Archives of Stephen Townroe
Part 15

The unique Bulleid diesel shunter working in Eastleigh East yard sometime between January 1951 and December 1952 and at the time around two years old. The main running lines are on the left and we are looking north towards Allbrook and Basingstoke. This was one of the few (possibly the only) visit this engine made to the Western Section of the Southern Region.

For the final instalment in the series we are in the period 1951 to November 1953 when the last entries relevant to the material available are made in SCT's b/w index. (He continued with b/w until about 1960 but these have not been located.) Post-1953 he was concurrently working with colour, indeed as we know he was an early exponent of colour and was fortunately able to record some quite unique scenes. (See 'SW Special No 10' devoted entirely to the work of SCT, which does not duplicate any of the views in the 'Lost Archive' series.)

The rest is probably best left to the images, 'the picture speaks the words' so to speak. However I cannot end this series without repeating my thanks to the Townroe family and Judith especially. Her willingness to assist and to respond to what I am sure she must have considered at times to have been seemingly pointless questions will forever be appreciated. Similarly her trust in loaning precious family papers without which none of this – nor indeed the book previously referred to – would have been possible to complete.

Perhaps the final word on SCT though should come not from me but from Hugh Davies of the Railway Enthusiasts Club (REC) at Farnborough who were extremely active in the 1950s promoting rail tours often involving unusual motive power not normally seen on particular routes.

The story begins when it came to the notice of the REC that an M7 and Beattie 'Well Tank' were concurrently under overhaul at Eastleigh. Around the same time an approach had been / was also made to Waterloo for one of these to be made available post- overhaul for a special train over the Bulford branch on 14 May 1955. Waterloo agreed and the choice was made for the 'Well Tank', again agreed by Waterloo.

The tour was duly confirmed; 'Andover Junction – Grateley – Bulford and return', seats offered and those who had booked looked forward to an interesting day out. But, literally just four or five days before the agreed date a further letter was received from Waterloo (everything then was of course arranged by post) which advised the selected engine was not available – it had in the meantime completed its overhaul and returned west to Exmouth Junction/ Wadebridge. A revised offer was made for the REC to have the newly overhauled M7 instead. This was hardly what the REC had wanted to hear but it appeared they had little choice; certainly commercially or indeed operationally there was little reason to bring the chosen engine back 100+ miles.

Even so, one of the REC members happened to mention this to SCT. Townroe was then at Eastleigh as District Motive Power Superintendent although of course Exmouth Junction and beyond was certainly not in his sphere of responsibility. All that need be said is that the REC got their engine, a case of not what you know but who you know, allied to the kindness and consideration of a man who was not only a senior railwayman but an enthusiast as well.

Above and opposite: **Re-railing C2X No 32522 just south of Midhurst on the line to Chichester, 24 February 1952 after its fall into a collapsed culvert following a period of heavy rain. Recovery was straightforward (well it was to SCT and the breakdown gang), as first of all the tender was removed, lightened somewhat as the water carried had all drained away, after which a ramp at 1-7 was dug out and the engine pulled back to the rails by 'pulling tackle'. Considering the strain being placed on the hawser it is perhaps surprising there are so many observers immediately adjacent. Notice the trilby-hat brigade in particular. Although seemingly battered the damage was superficial and after repair No 32522 survived in service until late 1961.**

Above and opposite: **Around the same time re-roofing of part (or was it all?) of the shed at Bournemouth took place seen here with an engineer's crane being used to lift the pre-assembled trusses into place whilst on the floor and leaning against the shed wall (interior views) are the cut components from the old roof. Servicing locomotives must have been difficult during the period although at least one engine, possibly a 'Lord Nelson', may be seen alongside the crane. The work was made more difficult by the presence of the supporting columns – again Health & Safety as witness the man stood on the top of the shed wall.**

Royal visit, Friday 21 November 1952. Her Majesty and entourage travelled by train to Fort Brockhurst and thence by road to visit the shore base HMS *Daedalus* at Lee-on-the-Solent. Notice the bunting wrapped around the candy-twist lamp standard! (Surely 'HM' would not have minded a bit of Southern green…) The return was from Fareham so we cannot be certain which of the two stations is seen here. The normal Special Traffic Notice for the week naturally gave only brief details of the Royal train but we are advised of the number of ordinary scheduled passenger and especially freight workings which were retimed or cancelled in consequence using the words 'Pathway not available'.

Something spoken of but rarely recorded on film. This is the SR's regional Mutual Improvement competition with the Traffic Manager Mr Chrimes (seated far left) in the chair. The location is not reported as neither are the identities of the others seen. Again from the current period previously mentioned.

Above: **A fitter in the process of servicing and fuelling LMS diesel No 10000 at Waterloo, 23 April 1953. The actual task would appear to be draining condensate from the fuel tank. SCT took three very similar views although regretfully the one with the actual fuelling hose connected was not of particularly good quality. Fuelling of the main line diesels at Waterloo was from a tank car positioned in the sidings on the south-east side of the station.**

Right: **The results of the broken driving axle on No 35020 in May 1953. Detail of this has been given elsewhere so not need be repeated in detail although suffice to say all the Merchant Navy class and later the Light Pacifics were inspected for similar flaws and indeed some were found, a case of 'just in time'. It was in consequence of this that various engines were hurriedly borrowed from the LMR and ER to cover the shortfall in motive power.**

Above and opposite: **Special train from Waterloo for the wedding of Lord Cameron and the Hon Mary Clare Douglas-Scoot-Montague seen at Beaulieu Road station with a headboard containing the respective families' coats of arms, 31 October 1953. Unfortunately the weather was far from kind as may be seen from the platform view. Frustratingly the identity of the 'Lord Nelson' at the head is not revealed with any certainty although from a poor view (not reproduced) the final digit of the number is certainly a '2', so either 30852 or 30862. The local *'Southern Daily Echo'* reported the merriment on its front page (alongside the headline of a local milkman being robbed after having been coshed by a bottle). Not sure about revised livery at the front end but it certainly stands out! The train ran from and returned to Waterloo. The outward journey leaving at 11.00 am and allowed an almost pedestrian 2hrs 29minutes for the Down journey with stops made at Basingstoke (3 minutes) and Southampton Central (4 minutes) en-route. Just four minutes were also allowed to detrain the passengers at Beaulieu Road, 1.33-1.37 pm, as running hot on its heels behind was the altered 11.30 am passenger service, retimed to depart at 11.35 am and which after leaving Southampton Central was non-stop to Brockenhurst. Meanwhile the special ran as ECS through to Bournemouth West again after a 3 minute wait at Bournemouth Central. The return left Bournemouth West Junction carriage sidings ECS at 4.40 pm (presumably with the same engine?), pausing at Bournemouth Central, Christchurch (working purposes..?) and Brockenhurst (water), before arriving back at Beaulieu Road at 5.40 pm. This time 17 minutes were allowed for the pick up and again with the same two stops for the Up journey. A final return to Waterloo was at 8.7 pm. The same source gives the formation as seven vehicles: BFK, TO, RF, TO, RF, TO, BFK.**

Opposite: **Two views of the same topic, one of which appeared in the** *Meccano Magazine* **for May 1954. They relate to an incident near Itchen Abbas as occurred on a Sunday in late November 1953 when the M7, No 30480, in charge of the Up pull-push Alton line service, broke a tyre on the right hand drive axle shortly after leaving the aforementioned station and whilst in the 'pushing' mode. It was one of these images that had first made me aware of SCT when I read the article for the first time some years later. As we know, the MM was aimed at the younger audience and so whilst technical details may have been lacking we are informed the train came to a stand 1½ miles west of Alresford. A replacement bus service was quickly provided whilst the breakdown crane was first taken from Eastleigh to Winchester where the hauling engine detached everything ahead of the crane itself, reattaching these to the rear and then proceeded to propel the entourage the six miles from Winchester along the Up main as far as Winchester Junction, and thence taking the Alton line to the scene of the breakdown. This procedure was necessary as the stricken engine had been running on the single line hence it was necessary to approach No 30480 head-on. Meanwhile SCT and the Foreman of the breakdown gang had gone ahead by car and upon arrival quickly decided on the best method of resolving the problem. Hence when the crane and fitters arrived, the rods were removed from the coupled wheels and the front of the engine then lifted. The tyre was then cut into three pieces which fell on to the lineside as the damaged axle was then rotated with the aid of a crowbar. Packing was then placed on the top of the axleboxes of the undamaged axle which when lowered back on to the track had the effect of raising the engine slightly so the now tyreless axle was clear of the track. The whole ensemble was then carefully and slowly towed back to Eastleigh, No 30480 running as an 0-2-4! Although SCT does not mention it, care would have had to be taken when passing under the various overbridges as the engine was now slightly higher at the front end than before. No 30480 was repaired at Eastleigh in the first days of December and returned to service for several more years until eventually retired in May 1964. Incidents such as these would have been the subject of internal reports prepared and kept at Eastleigh – or whichever shed/ depot was involved. At Eastleigh there were literally roomfuls of such paperwork on the floors underneath the water tank, rooms that had once been used as the dormitories years earlier. Sadly nearly everything from these archives were burnt, buried, destroyed, whatever, at the end of steam. 'Who would ever be interested in this sort of thing in the future?' was the comment of the time. Well I think we know the answer to that, as to be totally honest without SCT's short article in MM it would be another point of history likely forgotten for ever.**

Right: **Not from the same SCT archive but instead a confirmed Townroe view obtained from a different source and which fits in exactly here. This confirms the assertions in the previous caption and also provides for an overall view of the proceedings.**

Below: **We have few details of this image other than 'copy of colour transparency' 'train near Holmsley', clearly an M7 and another 'pull-push' working.**

The circumstances of the derailment of No 30854 at Shawford on 29 July 1952 has been covered in several journals previously. This views shows the engine upright again and ready to be towed back to Eastleigh for repair – damage was mainly superficial. SCT was at the time living just a matter of a few hundred yards from the scene whilst the event also occurred well within the area of his jurisdiction. We see here all (or some) of the Eastleigh breakdown gang responsible for the rerailing, this having been achieved by SCT instructing that rails be bolted to the wheels of the engine whilst it was lying on its side which when pulled upright would just need connecting to the rest of the network. Those right at the front are not identified with any certainty but would certainly be 'of a more senior grade'. (White is certainly not the colour for breakdown work!) Of the others, the tall man second in from the right with his elbow on the engine is Bill Bishop of Eastleigh.

Our final view is appropriately of the Townroe family. Mrs Townroe and daughters including twins on a visit to the Carriage Works at Eastleigh.

John Gayward Click
'Engineering the Southern' Part 2

More appropriate to Part 1 of this series, this is the first Merchant Navy, No 21C1 *Channel Packet*, on freight duty at Salisbury. Views such as this were widely circulated with the intention of deliberately depicting the type on freight duties, indeed to be fair they did haul prodigious freight loads over the Salisbury – Exeter route in their early years. (A case of 'we knew had an image like this but it was a bit too carefully 'filed''!)

If you are coming to this article 'cold', so to speak, a small amount of explanation is required. The memoirs of John Click are sadly incomplete whilst in addition there are on occasions several re-writes of specific pages, a few elaborations and, likely because of the missing pages, a few apparent contradictions. Neither are the originals kept in anything like date order.

The gaps are especially frustrating as we do not always have continuity. Consequently for Part 2 we have made the decision to concentrate solely on his experiences at Ashford, not necessarily chronological (although they are as near as possible in date order as we can achieve).

Consequently, for those wanting more on the Light Pacifics and Leader, do bear with us if we appear to have gone past the dates for these engines; have no fear at all, both are coming later during the time spent at Brighton and later at Eastleigh.

In Part 1 it will be recalled we left JGC depressed and concerned as to his own future. These feelings were clearly resolved for JGC affords a number of insights into his time at Ashford.

We start with the Q1 design and on which he does not really comment much (at this stage) although he notes, "When the Advertising Department photographer arrived at Ashford on 26 February 1942, the nearest he got to a complete Q1 was an engine with only a partial cab and the front buffers missing. In this form and with just inches to spare the 0-6-0 could be dealt with on the short pits at right angles to Ashford's main erecting shop. It was photographs of this design that made it look so toy like to some and prompted Stanier's enquiry about where to put the key!"

As if making excuses, later he described an apprentice-type prank involving another Q1, No C18. No date is mentioned but he 'mixes and matches' the number of the Q1 – C18 – with that of a BR engine, No 31069. We have left it as in the original text.

"Strange as it may seem to my readers I was not always old, and in my time I enjoyed a prank like most apprentices. One that was very tempting and easy to carry out presented itself when I was in the Erecting Shop at Ashford. No C18 had been under general repair and I had done the valve setting. Now the practice was for the engine, when completed, to be towed out (dead of course) by the Works' shunter – usually one of the 'R1' 0-6-0 tanks cut down for working the Canterbury and Whitstable line – for it to be reunited with its tender in the sidings alongside the main line at what was known as 'the old shed', about 350 yards from the shop doors.

With calculated innocence I deliberately left C18's valve gear in full back gear knowing the engine was going to get hauled out chimney first and that its steam reverser would be inoperable of course. Two other circumstances also had to be arranged; the regulator needed to be cracked open and the cylinder cocks closed. No 31069 came in to collect C18 and the shunter threw the 3-link coupling up on to the Q1's front hook. One of the perks on completing an engine was to ride on it out to 'The Shed'. I didn't do that, but walked alongside with Jimmy Deeley, a fellow apprentice who was in the know. This did not arouse any suspicion for there was no way of climbing up to

A member of the Q1 class under construction in 1942. On this occasion the location is Brighton. Of the 40 locos, the first 20 were built at Brighton and the remainder at Ashford.

the footplate anyway; the access steps were on the tender – a quarter of a mile away!

To start with it seemed the idea was not going to work, but after a surprisingly short distance the boiler pressure gauge was definitely rising; No C18 really was pumping herself up. The R1's driver, finding the going getting heavier, put on more steam. To our satisfaction there was about 85psi showing when, in order to do another job, the shunter decided to unhook C18 and leave her where she was for a minute, she wouldn't (shouldn't) be going anywhere, she had not been lit up.

He looked a bit puzzled as the coupling was tight, scratched his head and called "...ease up..." before managing to slip the coupling. Immediately she was released No C18 was off and with quite a powerful exhaust beat. Before it outstripped him the shunter threw his pole under the front wheels – a praiseworthy gesture but it made absolutely no difference. It was hilarious, Jimmy D collapsed in a heap of laughter as he often did, but I had miscalculated. The engine couldn't possibly get back, or could it? I had visions of it crashing through the now-closed doors back into the Shop it had just left. Thankfully it petered out about halfway back – phew!

When No 31069 went back and was hooked on once more. I'm ashamed to admit I said somewhat breezily, "That was dangerous – some twerp couldn't have thought what he was doing back there." Anyone who has had to get a locomotive into steam quickly will have used a version of this trick to pump

the boiler up with air so that the blower may be used before steam starts to be made. In our case the boiler was empty and the whole volume was an air vessel.

It was of course funny at the time but with hindsight a very stupid thing to have done – however a tenderless 'Q1' running backwards, cold, but under its own power, was at least different! OVB would definitely not have approved.

Sidney Lane was in charge at Ashford Shed, as true an example of a Motive Power officer as I ever knew; the butt of too many, but doing what he thought right just the same. I went the rounds for the first three months, including shift work with all the Running Foremen and absorbed the atmosphere thoroughly: this was the life.

The last three months were better still; I had a footplate pass for the Eastern Section and it was up to me to go where I wanted, to learn what I could and to do as much as I was allowed. It was stretching things a bit but I got as far as Bournemouth and Exeter! I think those three months were the happiest of my life. I already knew some enginemen, particularly Jack Chapman and his mate Don Pullen, who later became Assistant General Secretary of ASLEF, and with whom I'd enjoyed an illicit trip or two on 'King Arthurs'.

It was understood that I would go out with the breakdown train whenever a call came and I wondered how I would react to blood. Only one call came, fortunately without blood. We rushed up to Maidstone East as fast as a 'C' could take us and

A few years later E class 4-4-0 No 31166 is seen posed outside of Ashford shed in preparation for an RCTS railtour.

found the down line at the London end blocked by derailed coal wagons on the very edge of a long drop to the Medway below. Single line operation of London-bound electrics being in operation from the up bay. We summed up the situation. Sid Lane had one plan, his Mechanical Foreman another; and I was also asked what I'd do. To my astonishment, and his credit, Sid said we'd do it my way, which involved the 36-ton crane running back into the tunnel, which was on a curve, jib first and without its match truck. Its driver moaned but did what was required with great expertise. He backed out again, put the jib right up, turned through 180 degrees and we had the wagons back on very quickly. After that Sidney Lane urged me to go in for a job with Motive Power when I might have got a sub-shed of my own fairly quickly."

Later on JGC refers to venturing into the Shops at Ashford and it being an especially nasty shock after the Drawing Office. We know that after Ashford he moved to Brighton and spent some time in the Drawing Office; so clearly this was a return visit to Kent. He comments it was during the 1947 winter and the inside of the shops was only marginally better than being outside – the men having to break the ice in the washing up buckets.

One other unrelated matter which some may be unaware of was that on at least one occasion an engine from the RHDR came to Ashford for repair. This was around 1947 and was also the time Bulleid suggested to Captain J E P Howey that the Southern should build a pair of 15 inch gauge 'Merchant Navies' for the line although as we know this was not proceeded with. JGC comments that he worked on the RHDR 4-8-2 *Hercules* during its overhaul at Ashford and was involved with the valve gear during which time a visit was made by several of the 'top brass', this included Captain Howey, OVB, and A B Macleod (then the Southern Railway Stores Superintendent).

Around 1945 JGC transferred to the Brighton Drawing Office. With hindsight on history it was surely a wonderful

time. Bulleid's touch was ever present and as JGC and others put it, ideas just flowed on an almost continual basis. Not for Bulleid was there one moment when time stood still.

Some of this impetus may well have stemmed from his (OVB's) own time as an apprentice and here we are fortunate that JGC actually asked OVB of that time and equally reported the response. To quote JGC again, "In his most impressionable years, round the turn of the century, new designs emerged so frequently from the home railways alone that I once said to OVB how lucky he was to have been starting at such a time. "Oh, not a bit," he replied at once, "they were all exactly alike!" Now whilst that might patently be true of the brothers Drummond, for example, Holden's 'Decapod' experiment for the Great Eastern's intensive suburban services out of Liverpool Street really was quite sensationally different in 1902.

Line capacity on the GE was at saturation point and with electrification in the wind, Stratford designed a total adhesion 0-10-0 tank engine with the express (no, suburban!) aim of accelerating 300 tons of train to 30mph in 30 seconds from each station stop. It was a steam challenge that would give the kind of performance required today with electric services, but at a fraction of the first cost."

JGC continues, "Bulleid would have studied this design with great interest." But this is a hypothetical assertion by JGC for whilst it might appear likely Bulleid would have been well aware of the engine's existence, there is certainly no evidence to support it. The point is especially important later when considering how much Bulleid was aware of the Paget locomotive considering his (Bulleid's) subsequent use of the dry-back firebox and other features associated with Paget. Certainly as was the fashion then, general arrangement drawings of the 'Decapod' were published as soon as it was built. JGC continues again on the subject of OVB, "He would have approved of its large boiler having a Wootten firebox with no less than 48sqft of grate, noted the use of three cylinders and small wheels, all drivers, and wondered if the 80 ton weight on such a short wheelbase was practical or had in fact been achieved?" (The small amount of coal and water carried probably gave a clue about the last!) "It was compact in length and so could use existing run-rounds provided for existing 2-4-2 tanks."

"I failed to ask OVB if he ever saw the 'Decapod' and he probably didn't. It only existed in its 0-10-0 form from January 1903 until May 1904, for it was overweight, doubtless frightened the Civil Engineer who didn't want such a weight concentration at large, ran only a few tests and never entered revenue service. Bridge strengthening (already known to be needed before it was built) would have been essential for it to have worked regularly; but it did, with the help of automatic sanding during the 'take-off phase', achieve its designer's aim.

May we be forgiven for imagining OVB, having specially taken a day off during his apprenticeship, being lucky enough to see this monster hauling a string of eighteen coaches weighing 335 tons away from Chadwell Heath, its regular six exhaust beats merging into one roar before the tail of the train passed. "Acceleration superb" would have gone into his notebook: had he been there.

Holden's 'Decapod', more accurately described as the sole member of the Great Eastern Railway Class A55. The specification for the build was being able to accelerate 315 tons of train to 30 mph in 30 seconds. On test the engine more than exceeded this and according to Ahrons pulled a 335 ton train at the faster rate of 1.4 feet per second achieving this during inclement weather.

JGC mentions little about the build of the West Country class during his time at Brighton but here is an example of one of the engines built during his time. This example is No 21C135, later named *Shaftesbury,* and seen here on 27 August 1946 just a very few weeks since completion.

Alas, 'Decapod' was scrapped, though for decency's sake (and the accountants') it was claimed that another experimental locomotive, this time a tender 0-8-0, No20, was built from the parts in 1904-6; but that didn't last long either. James Holden's feelings are not on record. Nothing more was done so the Great Eastern had to soldier on until after WW2 resulting in a hoard of old, and some newer, small tankies dragging about the same decrepit stock that had so appalled OVB when Gresley had sent him to look it over after the amalgamation. The service was one of the wonders of the steam world in its day; the wonder being that it could be done at all."

At the same time as dealing with the 'might have beens' it may be appropriate to also deal with the Paget locomotive about which JGC passes a few similar comments. This is especially relevant to the subject in hand for 'Leader' would possess a number of similarities with this engine and we cannot therefore have doubt that OVB was aware of it. JGC also adds his own unique perspective to this aspect of history.

"The Midland Railway in the first decade of this century was a line where

4-4-0s ran most expresses whilst 0-6-0s predominated on freight work. Double heading was so rife, so ingrained and so uneconomic that the Derby Works Manager, Paget, decided to

do something about it. In a private office in Derby he started the design of a large general purpose locomotive which would be far superior to anything at work at that time, would eliminate the double heading and yet be an engineman's engine, easy to work on and easy to maintain: a quantum leap ahead! Paget's standing, his boldness and, he trusted, his finances, too were such that he proposed nothing less than getting his wonder machine designed, built and into service entirely on his own initiative; quite apart from Deeley being the CME and his boss! One suspects that Deeley, far from happy with the arrangement, was unable to resist strong influence – from some of the Midland directors possibly? In any event Paget saw two employees, Chambers and Clayton, each evening after his usual day spent running the Works. Clayton especially is very much part of our story for after helping Paget and spending time with the Midland he returned to Ashford whence he had come. By the time Maunsell retired he had long been his Personal Assistant. Bulleid inherited him, of course, and it was then that he heard a detailed account of Paget's work for the first time. OVB was impressed and gave Clayton every encouragement to set down a complete record of the Paget saga; complete, that is, from the time the original design for a 4-6-0 gave way to the 2-6-2 that was as actually built and carrying the number 2299.

The original 4-6-0 on which Paget's Patents* were based was rather different and Clayton had fortunately brought a general arrangement blueprint of it with him, but must have forgotten where he put it. Subsequently at Brighton in 1950 I was asked to clear 'rubbish' from a cupboard; and, in doing so, opened a large blueprint of Paget's 4-6-0. *(JGC now states, "It was saved from oblivion, probably all that remains of that design." Unfortunately the question is now, "Saved to where?" as there was no trace of it amongst the JGC archive.)* I'm sure Bulleid didn't see the drawing, or he might have dallied with some of its more radical details. Even so there were similarities with 'Leader'. The Paget 4-6-0 had eight single-acting cylinders supplied by two sleeve valves, although they were arranged vertically rather than horizontally and driven, curiously enough, by chains. Mechanically its most bizarre feature was the system of inside coupling rods which helped balancing but was wisely rejected for the 2-6-2 eventually built in favour of ordinary outside rods. The 4-6-0's boiler had a cylindrical, corrugated firebox very similar to the ones Hoy had fitted to some of his 0-8-0s for the L& YR shortly before.** The idea in each case was to get rid of stay problems by eliminating them altogether; a very natural reaction to a particularly nasty boiler explosion on the L& Y***. Paget eliminated stays on his 2-6-2 by using a brick-lined firebox without any water-legs at all; a decision that greatly simplified fire cleaning and ash disposal – a lesson that Derby failed to learn but took to its heart years afterwards from the Yankee S160 2-8-0s. At no point in his account does Clayton refer to trouble with the brick lining of the firebox though Paget himself told Kenneth Leech that cracking trouble did occur, and must have potentially been very serious.

* The Patent office lists three relevant patents lodged by Cecil Walter Paget, firstly in 1901 under the bland title 'Locomotive', then in 1902 'Improvements in Locomotives' and finally in 1913 with 'Improvements in Valves for Steam and other Engines.' Potentially the most interesting of these is likely to be the first but, regretfully, whilst an abstract is available for the 1902 and 1913 inventions nothing is available for the 1901 listing. With the drawing referred to by JGC in 1950 seemingly having been lost to history, it appears that yet again any chance of locating further information on the Paget designs has once again been thwarted.

** There is some reference to Henry Hoy and his firebox design on Wikipedia: https://en.wikipedia.org/wiki/Henry_Hoy

*** Here the reader is referred to the book 'Locomotive Boiler Explosions' by C H Hewison, David & Charles 1983 and 2003. Chapter 7, pages 110 to 113, refer to various boiler/ firebox explosions that occurred to engines on the L& Y in the early years of the twentieth century although it does not seem possible to specifically relate to the one particular case referred to in the text.

The subject of footplate riding is something JGC talks about on a number of occasions in his memoirs, most notably how when allocated an Eastern Section pass he managed to extend its use on to the Western section as far as Exeter. If he had been out, one response that might have worked was 'initiative'! The view seen here showing No 21C13 *Blue Funnel* having just backed on to its train at Waterloo with the crew and engine receiving some envious comments from the admirers.

Did the Midland invent individual costing for the Paget job? Quite likely, but it is a sad fact that Paget's personal money ran out before No 2299 was completed and he had no option but to ask for financial help on the Midland's terms which put limits on the amount of testing work to be involved.

With so much that was new it was inevitable that plenty of teething troubles were met. Thermal expansion problems with the sleeve valves were never cured, nor really likely to be cured, because if they were made steam-tight when cold, they seized when hot; but when 'eased' to get over that problem they leaked so badly when cold that the locomotive could not be seen for steam! *(Again an exact repeat of what would occur later with No 36001.)* Nevertheless the loco did run, well and fast, and was kind to the track. Unfortunately on one of these runs No 2299 wrecked its vitals *(JGC's words)* and caused a major delay when the sleeve valves seized up solid one Sunday at 70mph. After that it didn't run again and lay under dust sheets in Derby Paint Shop until, with Paget safely away in charge of the Railway Operating Division in France and every bit of space wanted for the war effort, 'Paget's Folly', as it was known, was cut up.

"When I asked OVB if he ever know Paget personally he said no, but he did know him at that time in France. It must have taken a lot for him to speak as he did for Bulleid sympathised with the French who couldn't stand (Lieutenant Colonel) Paget, "… he would range up and down behind the front in his personal train reorganising everything in sight. On one occasion he arrived at Amiens and offered to show the French how to shunt their yard: being them, they politely agreed. After Paget eventually turned in for the night the French made a very rough shunt on to his sleeping car. He was off next morning and we didn't see him again for months."

After the War, Paget put his wartime traffic experiences into practice to very good effect back on the Midland, but left locomotive design to the stay-at-home Derby die-hards. *(This is contradicted on Wikipedia where his biography refers to him not having returned to the railway post-WW1.)* Understandably No 2299 was taboo until Clayton revealed nearly all in 1945 when he remembered Paget as a great man whose ideas ought to have had more impact on the future of steam traction.*

"What a pity neither Paget nor Clayton ever discussed the engine with Bulleid. 'Leader' might then not have incorporated some of its worst faults." *(More likely there was simply not the opportunity. By the time Bulleid had got around to considering several of the features of the Paget machine which were subsequently incorporated in 'Leader', Paget was no longer alive – he died in 1936. Clayton too had died in October 1946.)*

But history does repeat itself, for the true *'raison d'etre'* of Bulleid's 0-6-6-0 was remarkably similar to the Decapod's, whilst many of Paget's ideas were updated and re-used at Brighton. *(At this point one would expect an objective comment to have been made along the lines of 'How and why did Bulleid believe he could succeed where Paget had failed?'*

Even if we allow Bulleid the benefit of failing to know about the Paget machine from years past he surely would have been alerted to the article by Clayton in 1945. Was Bulleid's persistence then a genuine belief he could do better or simply stubbornness?)

At this stage JGC's career path again becomes confused. We know he was in the Drawing Office for a time and later went to the Testing Section under H W Attwell – apologies then if things are slightly out of order. He may even have moved between the two and back again. *(200+ pages of notes/ duplications/re-writes, and undoubtedly some gaps as well, have taken some sorting.)*

With the Testing Section at Brighton

"If there was one thing I became convinced of in the Shops it was that a yawning gap existed between works' repairs and locomotive running. I think that first came home to me when repairing exhaust injectors. The sheds sent them in as 'defective' and only ever got a 'dud' back in exchange; because, although we sent repaired ones up for testing, they never worked as intended! I took a strong objection to exhaust injectors and was very glad that Bulleid's engines weren't saddled with them.

Every Monday morning a string of locomotives was shunted over to the Works for repair and, if one had arrived overnight from its home shed it would, with any luck, still have enough steam in it to work injectors or to create vacuum. In that way I got some practice that would be useful later on.

I began to think about what I wanted to do after the apprenticeship was over and there seemed to be three alternatives: to go back to the Drawing Office, to join Motive Power, or to get involved with test work. To keep the options open I went every single week to the Chief Clerk, Chittenden, to try to get 'six months at the Shed'; considered a great prize. He was always very helpful and my persistence eventually worked.

We did quite a lot of test work on Q1s and one was particularly tedious. Somebody had arrived at Waterloo with a 'brilliant' design of driving axlebox made in two halves with a vertical joint down the middle – looking on the end of the axle – the two halves held together by four strong horizontal bolts.

OVB was entranced and fell for it straightaway. Mechanical lubrication was, surprisingly, not essential; but the attractive theory was the absence of a break in the bearing surface anywhere; and, since oil would be arriving constantly, it wouldn't matter that there was no oil reservoir except in the carefully machined oil grooves.

About six of them were done, and every time one ran hot (and they did frequently) it meant a miserable day at Feltham or Guildford looking for the precise cause which was either no oil or too little and too late; there was just no way of being sure. The only sure thing would be a reprimand 'for not being sure'.

* *Reference James Clayton 'The Paget Locomotive' published in The Railway Gazette, 2 November 1945, and subsequently also produced as a booklet.*

JGC does not refer to a specific member of the Q1 class that was the subject of the axlebox trials, but elsewhere he does make mention of his fondness for the J class 0-6-4T but without explaining why. In appearance the design displayed a marked familiarity with the H class 0-4-4T but here any similarity ended for the J was a much larger machine with correspondingly higher tractive effort. Elsewhere in his text, Click refers to individuals by name or initials. Where the identity of these persons is definitely known we have included the full identification, otherwise the initials are left as written.

We would check the mechanical lubricator, the pipes and hose, do our best for the journal, re-metal the box, bore it to recommended clearances, chip and scrape the grooves by hand, put the box together, replace the axle, couple up and prime the pump until oil was seen squeezing out, and Bob's your uncle until next time; but that could, depressingly, be on the very next trip. Then another failure was chalked up, the availability figure went down and we started all over again. I hated them. I might add that the Works did too; their 'new out' results were indistinguishable.

OVB was said to be particularly keen in making a 'go' of this 'experiment' as he preferred to call it; but, try as we might, nobody did. It was very difficult to feel one was doing much good on such occasions.

Only years later did I read that the Eastern & North Eastern regions actually fitted some A1 Pacifics with these boxes and had identically worse results, if you'll forgive that description.

The run-of-mill activity was to go to a shed and wade through repair cards looking for evidence of work done on a test fitting, and then try to get the foreman fitter to remember what precisely he had done because the entry was quite meaningless to us both. I think OVB must have done work just like this himself at one stage – for he set great store by investigating repair books and bade us do likewise. It was broadly good experience. One later test I liked was on a Lord Nelson, No. 30851 *Sir Francis Drake*; and I liked it not because it concerned an exhaust injector (though it was a much improved 'J' class one) but for where the engine worked in and out of: Southampton Docks. There was always something new to see, if one could stand the heart rending scenes at No11 platform at Waterloo as families of emigrants *(the '£10 Poms' who emigrated to Australia around this time)* tore themselves apart for ever.

One day No 30851 could have cost me my life. He, she or it had worked up in the morning and was going back to Eastleigh light engine. It looked like, and was, a good test of the injector which we would be frequently having to change over due to the light working. As we sped down on a whiff of steam the injector wasted hardly a drop, performing exactly as it should. The firedoor was wide open as we approached Pirbright where there is a short 'tunnel' (under the Basingstoke canal) with individual bores for each road. We plunged in and a huge flame the diameter of the firehole blew back over the tender top. I instinctively turned my back on it and saw the unquenched flame disappearing down beyond the back of the tender! If one of us had been in its way there would have been no chance. It was just the situation that was very much a possibility in the 'Leaders' central cab when running chimney first.

Friends at Bournemouth would, if not asked too often, put one of their 'Nelsons' on the through train they worked to Oxford and back, via Reading West curve and Didcot, involving a trot down the Great Western main line, of course. I would go down to Southampton, join the locomotive there, go through to Oxford and then back to Basingstoke with the return working.

Why? The Nelsons had a very long copper inner firebox and differential expansion caused constant problems with leaking tubes. Long term tests went on with one half of the small tubes rolled straight into the tubeplate whilst the other had ferrules. Working the engine hard and then going on the shed, as at Oxford, was enough to set off serious leakage; not always, yet sometimes rivalling Niagara Falls. The problem had to be lived with, and was a feature of the design that caused difficulties with staying as well. Opinions were divided as to which arrangement was the better and the question was never resolved.

It was always novel, and inconvenient to say the least, to find all the Western's signals on the wrong side!"

No 30851 this time leaving Waterloo on a Bournemouth – Waterloo train and not the light engine trip described in this article. Readers will be aware there is a vast archive of photographs taken by John Click and deposited at the National Railway Museum. Unfortunately the required costs for searching/copying and reproduction prohibit their use. *S C Nash/SLS*

No. 850 *Lord Nelson* on trial with indicator shelter. This type of trial, seeing engineers crouched at the front, was another role of the Testing Section.

Back in time some years and JGC gives an insight into Bulleid's first impression of a member of the 'Lord Nelson' class on the road. This was 20+ years before JGC's referred-to trip to Oxford described above and is especially interesting in the way Bulleid is described, reference his note taking. Bulleid was still with the LNER at this time and the trip was (according to JGC) no doubt arranged between the two CMEs (Gresley and Maunsell) at a Meeting of the Association of Railway Locomotive Engineers. What neither he nor Bulleid explain is why the journey was made in the first place. Was Maunsell keen to show off his creation, was Gresley (or Bulleid) curious, or was Maunsell seeking an impartial opinion from an outside individual rather than a member of his own staff?

JGC again. "Bulleid always said that a helpful method of judging ride quality was to write notes and compare their legibility. That seems to be borne out by those he made in 1927 when he rode on Maunsell's *Lord Nelson*, then just over a year old and still undergoing service trials before more were ordered. *(Bulleid was also involved in the riding trials of a 'River' class engine following the Sevenoaks disaster of 1927, but we do not know which footplate experience came first.)* Whenever the locomotive was running fast, yet "not really moving" as he might have put it, the writing then gets a bit groggy! Going down they had a 425 ton 'Golden Arrow' rake; but the return train, the 2.30pm Ostend up, was of only 277 tons. Perhaps that was why his notes afterwards stated:-

"The engine was never worked to any power, and appears to be too powerful for the work it is doing. The blast action on the fire was very steady indeed and no sparks were thrown. Boiler pressure was maintained, in fact care was taken to prevent the engine blowing off frequently. The engine was driven on the regulator" – cut off was a uniform 25% throughout. "The exhaust injector was in use most of the time

to maintain the water level. The tender rides extremely well but the design of the coal space is bad – the coal not feeding forward. Smoke and steam beat down badly"; smoke deflectors were not fitted until 1929. "The fireman found the long grate rather difficult and had to push the fire forward four times." I can imagine OVB dodging the dreadfully long, and hot fire irons." *(Clearly JGC had access to the notes of the time, regretfully he makes no mention of this type of recording elsewhere. What a treasure trove they would surely be if they have/ had survived.)*

"The fireman that day was Royal Train Driver Philpot. By the time he recounted this tale in the 1950s he mentioned that when OVB had ridden with them "he condemned the engine!" At least OVB put the coal problem right when he got the chance a decade later. Apart from investigating the riding qualities, Bulleid's particular interest would have been in this 4-cylinder loco's 135 degree crank setting (giving eight exhaust beats per driving wheel revolution) and in its general performance remembering it featured long lap and high superheat – the latter not employed on the 'Castle' that had shocked King's Cross in the 1925 exchanges. He seems not to have spotted the deficient exhaust arrangements on this trip – the worst shortcoming of the Nelsons as built – but he put that right too later."

Dynamometer Cars

"OVB would never comment in any detail about the humiliating 1925 locomotive exchange when a 'Castle' showed Gresley's Pacifics a thing or two – it must have been a taboo subject at King's Cross – but he liked to tell a later tale against the 'Royal Scots'. The LMS were very pleased with them, and who wouldn't be compared with the 'Claughtons', but when

As is known, the Southern never did possess its own Dynamometer Car, indeed until the exchange trials of 1948 we do not know of any occasion when a vehicle was borrowed. After this time there is recorded use of the LNER car during the 1950 trails of Leader, another car a few years later with some of the Bulleid main line diesels and later still in 1956 when a further unspecified car was used to test the performance of the first rebuilt Merchant Navy. The LNER car is seen here at Banbury, presumably heading back home in late August 1950 after the first series of trials with No 36001 in August 1950.
Steve Banks collection

they published figures for coal consumption per drawbar horsepower hour that were so low that neither Gresley nor he could believe them, Bulleid thought of a plan.

OVB commented, "I got Gresley to ring Sir Henry (Fowler) and say that our dynamometer car was unserviceable so could he possibly please lend us his. Of course he affably agreed. I then arranged for the two cars (the NER car and the L& Y one) to be coupled together at their business ends and proceeded to pull them apart using a turnbuckle whilst noting the readings in both."

As expected, a big difference was found. Gresley was very pleased, the more so because he had by then obtained much better figures from one of his Pacifics, altered, on Spencer's recommendation, to have long-lap valves. It was very clear that Fowler's figures were wishful thinking.

To be on the safe side OVB carefully calibrated their car using deadweights applied to the drawbar via a bell-crank, which confirmed its accuracy. I never liked to ask did he apply the same deadweight test to the LMS car too.

All this really was Bulleid at his naughty best; the more so because the story, as told, led me to think that Fowler was left happily oblivious of the error. It also confirms the human weakness for believing, as all concerned here did, what they wanted to believe.

Drawing Office tales

At Brighton we normally had nothing at all to do with tenders, nor did the Waterloo people, it was the Ashford office that prepared the plans. The design of the tenders for the lightweights were finished long before the locomotive; and at 8ft 6ins wide could have been used for more Q1s or for any of several alternatives that got looked at. It was the more puzzling therefore when I was told to "…get out a drawing of the rear end of one of the first ten 'Merchant Navy' class showing everything from the front of the firebox back to the middle axle of the tender". We couldn't think what it was wanted for and the best guess was that it was a blank on which the hose connections between engine and tender could be looked at again; a devil of a job and one best done on the actual locomotive if there was time. We were told that the drawing had been checked at Waterloo and heard nothing more. Only months later when No 35005, as it by then was, emerged from Eastleigh after a General Repair did I realise that my drawing had gone to the States for Berkeley's to scheme out how their mechanical stoker could be arranged.

By 1944 Bulleid wanted his future Pacifics to be more simply styled. He asked for the level of the bottom line of the casing over the driving wheels to be carried right along the loco; no pretty curves as on *Channel Packet*. Churchward might have let Holcroft add them to his 'Stars': OVB would go the other way. Larman and I were horrified – the cylinders and the firebox side would be visible – so we wrote and signed a note to the great man asking if he would think again. CSC must have been sympathetic for word came back that plates could be added, but not with curves. The plates got fitted, but when OVB was shown

the painting diagrams he insisted on black below the casing – right along the tender too. They looked high and racy. Years afterwards, in about 1960, I was talking to R G Jarvis in his office when Eddie Standen requested audience full of a sorry tale that drivers were not attending to the bogie lubrication because they had to duck under the plate ahead of the cylinders to get at an oil pot. "Do you mean that we should remove this plate?" Jarvis said. "Um – yes," and it was done. Bulleid would have approved; but it did spoil the look of the first ten. It was a pity no reason was found to take off the other piece.

One day I was called in to CSC's office: wondering what I had done. "Are yer King Arthur?" I must have looked astonished. The question was asked again, "Are yer KING ARTHUR?" "Aw naw,I curl see yer not!" He then explained that "The Chief is very annoyed". A note, and I'd seen it, had appeared in the *Railway Magazine*, under this *nom de plume*, to the effect that the 'lightweights' were being designed "to go over Meldon Viaduct". It was a lapse in security of the kind OVB wouldn't tolerate. Larry L., the other prime suspect, was questioned similarly before it was concluded that 'King Arthur' worked for the Chief Civil Engineer who had only agreed 18t 15cwt as the maximum axle-weight he could accept over Meldon shortly before. A letter of complaint would have gone to Cantrell. (This was not dissimilar when it is recalled how the young Ian Allan produced his ABC of Southern locomotives and was vilified by OVB as to how dare anybody publish details without his permission.)

Frequently there would be a particular 'flap' on in the DO involving a whole section. An example was when, quite late in the design of the 'lightweights', OVB asked for a full rock/drop grate to be fitted. The S160s (the 2-8-0s of the USA Transportation Corps) had by then had a marked effect on Derby's design ideas and Bulleid heard all about their latest grates, probably from brother-in-law H G Ivatt. Led by CSC, Frank Crouch, Dick Barnes and Peter Cooper, a couple of days were spent 'brainstorming' the problem. A principal source was the 1944 Edition of the American "Locomotive Cyclopedia" which was very well thumbed, I can tell you. A main problem was the unavoidable extra weight, and the American examples looked hefty in the extreme. Unfortunately the compromises worked out with weight saving in view caused the whole arrangement to be rather too flimsy, and it gave a lot of trouble in service later on.

In a case like this I couldn't understand why someone didn't go and physically look at an S160, roll his sleeves up and use the facilities to dispose of a 'boxful of clinker and ash'. Better still, why not set to and deal with six locomotives a day for a week. If that didn't suggest improvements nothing would. This is being wise after the event with a vengeance; people simply didn't do that sort of thing then, even if they may have done in Maunsell's time.

Too often, I think, failure to appreciate the real life, down-to-earth situations weakened our designs. This obviously was an example where close liaison with Motive Power was badly needed, but it never happened in any constructive way at the design stage; nobody was assigned to do it. Bulleid didn't insist on it and Motive Power never asked; or perhaps they did!

Meldon viaduct with a WR diesel. Ignore the diesel and instead focus on the structure...the reference to 'King Arthur' earlier in the text thus becomes clear.

Even so, the S160s did influence British design quite a lot, but Bulleid thought them unnecessarily complicated compared with his 'Ql' and that was partly true. He liked, and did it often, to compare engine diagrams by having overlay tracings made. A coloured print added to his personal loco diagram book, which is in front of me now *(again, what happened to this?),* is the case in point. A 'Q1' is superimposed in red on an S160 and in size and capacity for work both are remarkably similar. The main differences one sees are that the Yankee has more axles, it has compensated springing on the driving wheels and a much lower axle-weight than the 'Q1' making it far more suitable for the poor track conditions that would be found behind the front in Europe. The American also has a steel inner firebox whereas the Q1 is of copper. In view of the unusual measures taken to reduce the Q1's weight, it is surprising that Bulleid didn't go for a steel box as well. The reason must lie in the haste with which the job was done rather than in any second thoughts about the steel fireboxes in the first ten 'Packets', though those boxes by then were beginning to give trouble.

Not only was the Q1 boiler directly related to the Lord Nelson, but its closer relative still was the boiler designed originally for the 'Schools' class. That boiler (a 'half-Nelson' if you like, but more nearly two-thirds) was still in the drawers at Eastleigh and it provided the jumping-off point. The boiler actually fitted to the 'Schools' was developed from the round topped 'King Arthur' boiler when it was realised that the first boiler, besides being too heavy, would make the drivers' view from the tumblehome cab (needed to clear the Hastings line gauge) very poor indeed because of the protruding corner of the Belpaire. Design, all design, is an evolutionary process.

R G Jarvis told me that at Derby when a design problem cropped up, to which there was not an immediate solution, the inevitable question was..."what did we do on the Compound?" whereupon the appropriate drawing would be unearthed, consulted and, possibly, be copied or updated. It was very similar with us: how did we do it on the 'Schools'? (I'd back the 'Schools' any day!) Later on it became what did we do on the 'West Country'?

Bulleid's Coaches

A start had also been made on new locomotive-hauled coaches but the war prevented them getting beyond the underframe stage. Surprisingly, these were stored until 1944 rather than getting snapped up for some kind of war use. Bodies were built and complete coaches came out from late 1945, but were something of a hybrid owing quite a lot, including length, to the Maunsell era though they did exhibit a Bulleid speciality, the attractive curved, flush sides.

The first truly post-war main line coach, a prototype of course, came out in the summer of 1945 and looked marvellous. It was on a new standard underframe that made the vehicle no less than 67' 1" over buffers. It was also singularly clean-lined with large windows in the curved sides that OVB had already made his own both in locomotives and earlier vehicles. The new design was shown to the public for their democratic view on, mainly, whether compartment or open stock should be built in future. It even had electric underfloor foot warmers, a clear indication, even then, that OVB was feeling the effects of hypothermia (JGC's word), much to the benefit of his fellow sufferers. This prototype and all subsequent varieties of Bulleid's steam-hauled stock had steel-clad, wooden-framed bodies; and when asked why, LI Sanders said that unlike the suburban stock the numbers didn't justify the changeover.

When BR Standard Mk.1 coaches came out they did have steel bodies but still on separate underframes. In my view, and it is shared by many, the Bulleid stock was imitated in the Mk.ls, yet the latter never quite achieved the sheer style that Bulleid did. His wife Marjorie, whom I never had the pleasure of meeting, often advised on decor and she must have had very good taste.

It must be said though that Bulleid was constantly trying to change details and it was much to the credit of those running the carriage works that any two vehicles emerged alike. A ploy, certainly used advantageously in Ireland to mitigate this problem, was for a compartment mock-up to be always available on which OVB could try curtains, carpets, lighting, upholstery and fittings to his heart's content, changing it every time he came down, and the more the better, whilst the production team just carried on with the building!

Now for the faux pas. Who started the Tavern Car idea? I can't think it was OVB himself although the inside was a novelty that had commercial possibilities. I truly think he must, quite flippantly and without the slightest idea that he would be taken up on it, have said something, to Shepherd perhaps, about the outside painting and hadn't the heart to say no when it got done: nothing else fits. Missenden was non-committal at first and had them shared out round the regions, but wavered in his support and then capitulated to the pressure when 'influential gentlemen' on the 'Master Cutler' said enough was enough to *The Times* no less. I couldn't resist including the shot of the interior of the restaurant car that went with each twin set, the turnover rate at times of high demand for lunch or dinner was just what was wanted, but it does look remarkably like a lord mayor's banquet set out in a mobile chicken coop.

The most handsome vehicles of all were those six-car sets for the Bournemouth line; whilst, for the most novel, we need to go back to a single vehicle, No 100s, built as a sleeping car for the Southern Directors in which almost everything was new and different. For its inspiration we need to go back still further to wartime boat building.

During the war Bulleid had asked to be allowed to build launches at Eastleigh, "the biggest and the best" for preference, but things were a bit limited by the need to go out of the shop doors and then travel to their true element (water) by flat wagon. Now from the earliest recorded times boat builders had built upwards from a keel; but, no, OVB had different ideas. He would, and did, achieve better results by jigging the hulls upside down and putting the keels on last. The slight problem of turning them over afterwards was of no consequence; though the Admiralty Commissioner, after recovering from apoplexy, did point out that the method might not catch on for battle cruisers.

No 100s then was built like his boats, the two halves of the resin-bonded plywood body were united at the top by a keel-like ridge member, whilst the lower sides met the underframe; making, for the first time, an inherently stable structure: beautiful. The rest of the dividing walls between compartments went in rather like the formers in a wooden aircraft, such as the Mosquito. The plumbing was well thought out, if not cleaned out, and Bulleid decided to take a shower, without knowing he was performing its christening rites before breakfasting with his fellow officers.

A B MacLeod, who was Stores Superintendent, and aboard, said he only once saw OVB really angry; and he had cause, after all, for the shower spluttered and issued forth a mixture of cold water, oil, copper swarf and pellets of solder. I saw this vehicle several times, in the up bay at Ashford, coupled to a similarly re-profiled utility van which had a noisy generator inside to supply essential services when parked in an otherwise quiet siding for the night. It became known that Sir Cyril Hurcomb considered No 100s the most comfortable vehicle he ever slept in. I chanced once to say this to my second cousin Percy Bennell. He roared with laughter; "HURcomb," he kept saying, – "he is in charge of the Transport Commission?" They had both joined the Civil Service together: "Pooh-Bah," Elliot calls him, so perhaps all in all he wasn't the best witness. Seriously again, the other most interesting feature was 100s' bogies – centreless and developed from those first used under the Co-Co electric, the first CC1. It became a pet idea of Bulleid's but his Technical Assistant L Lynes, whom I only knew by sight, was against it, as they were in Ireland when he introduced it experimentally there later on."

Next time: The sometimes genuinely hilarious time with No 36001…

And finally for this instalment, an example of a Bulleid coach, corridor brake composite, at Clapham Yard in the early 1950s. *Amyas Crump*

Knowle Halt

Roger Simmonds

nowle Hospital (formerly the Hampshire County Asylum) was opened on 13 December 1852 and was the first such institution in the County. It was later supplemented by Park Prewett Mental Hospital in Basingstoke (1917), St James Hospital in Portsmouth (1879), and Whitecroft, on the Isle of Wight, as the need for psychiatric care increased.

It came into being as a result of the requirement to comply with the 1845 Lunacy Act, the County of Southampton (sic) required to provide asylum accommodation for lunatics within its care and the site chosen was at Knowle Farm between Fareham and Wickham.

A plan drawn up by the appointed surveyor James Harris, for the site, incorporated a corridor plan structure integrating the usual service areas behind a grand administration block separating male and female wings, and became a model for other similar asylums. Soon after opening in 1852 demand for space meant that extensions were necessary, with these added to both ends and south fronts of both male and female wings. Further extensions took place around 1870 when a separate three storey block for "*Chronic lunatics and idiots*" was constructed south of the main frontage to free up space for "*Curable lunatics*" in the main building.

The southern boundary of the site lined the London and South Western Railway's Eastleigh to Fareham Line although at that time little thought was given to making use of the convenient rail connection. By 1900 however there seems to have been an unofficial arrangement revealed in a letter from the Hants County Asylum to the LSWR on 12 December requesting the issue of "*cheap tickets for visitors who travel on the last Wednesday in each month and are set down at the Asylum*". At the time this request was declined but with the caveat that this request would be reviewed "*when the Meon Valley line is opened*".

On 28 November 1906 a report from the LSWR Superintendent of the Line referred to the "*long standing custom of stopping trains on certain days at Knowle Junction for the convenience of persons visiting the Hants County Asylum*". He recommended that a small platform be constructed "*alongside the existing line which is now being provided for Meon Valley trains*", the cost being estimated at £53. He concluded that it "*could also be used by members of the Asylum staff who have recently applied for such facility*".

Following approval, the LSWR wrote to the Board of Trade on 22 May 1907 confirming the new works in the location which included the new independent line through the old Fareham Tunnel serving Meon Valley trains and the new

Knowle Halt in BR days. Views of the location in LSWR/ Southern times are conspicuous by their absence but it is reasonable to assume that seen here is a Southern Railway replacement including their standard use of concrete. The siding referred to may just be glimpsed in the background. (Funtley Brickworks private siding was further south towards Fareham but again only able to be accessed from the single line.)

platform at Knowle Halt. Major Pringle duly appeared on 8 June to inspect the various new works associated with the Meon Valley line. The part of his report specific to Knowle is as follows:

"A new siding connection for the County Asylum has been laid connected to the single line for Meon Valley trains facing the Fareham direction. The points are worked from a 5 lever ground frame of which 1 lever is spare. The ground frame is controlled by the Fareham East to Wickham train tablet. The interlocking is correct."

It is interesting that this is the first reference to provision of a siding at Knowle not to be confused with the nearby siding laid in serving Funtley brickworks, also inspected at this date. Major Pringle then addressed the new Halt:

"In addition a platform has been erected on private ground adjoining Knowle siding. This is for use of employees of the County Asylum and visitors and is not advertised in Bradshaw. It has a length of about 100 feet, a width of 9 feet and a height of 3 feet. As it is not intended for use after dark, no provision for lighting has been made. But I understand during winter months the platform will be used after dark by the asylum attendants and in this case it will be necessary to provide lamps. This the company undertook to do and stairs are also to be erected as a better means of access to the platform. In the circumstances I see no objection to the use of this platform."

A subsequent letter from the LSWR to the BoT dated 20 September confirmed that lighting had now been provided, notably 'electric powered' lamps were installed thus making Knowle one of the earliest rural stations on the LSWR system to be so fitted. Interestingly the electricity was supplied by the hospital generator. Possibly owing to increased use of the platform, Hants County Asylum wrote again to the LSWR on 7 January 1909 requesting the provision of a shelter on the platform. This was agreed at an estimated cost of £71 with the Asylum Committee paying half the cost. This then represents the final form of the facilities at Knowle Halt through to the 1950s.

Some interesting operational snippets can be gleaned from official documents. The 1921 LSWR Working Timetable Appendix for example states that passengers intending to alight at Knowle Halt will be accommodated in the rear of the train. The 1934 Southern Railway WTT Appendix enlightens us further:

*"**Knowle Asylum Halt** – No staff are provided at the platform, and, except when otherwise arranged, Guards of trains stopping at the platform must note the number of passengers joining the trains and see that their fares are collected at the termination of their journey. The Guards, except when otherwise arranged, will also be responsible for the collection of tickets from passengers alighting. These tickets must afterwards be delivered up at Wickham or Fareham station, as the case may be, for despatch to the Audit Office in the usual way."*

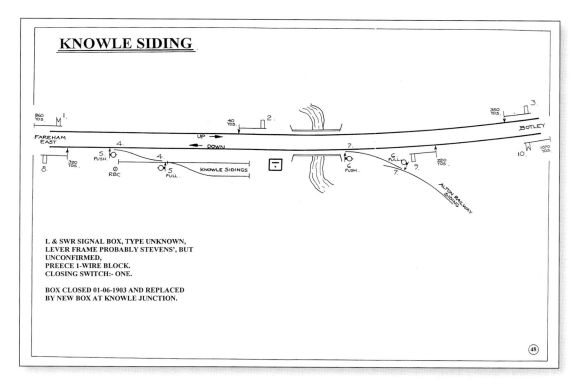

Courtesy of the excellent George Prior 'Signal Box Diagrams' Vol 15.) The first shows the connections as existed prior to the opening of the Meon Valley line. At this stage a signal box was provided to facilitate and control contractors traffic off the MV line and which also covered the Knowle siding connection.

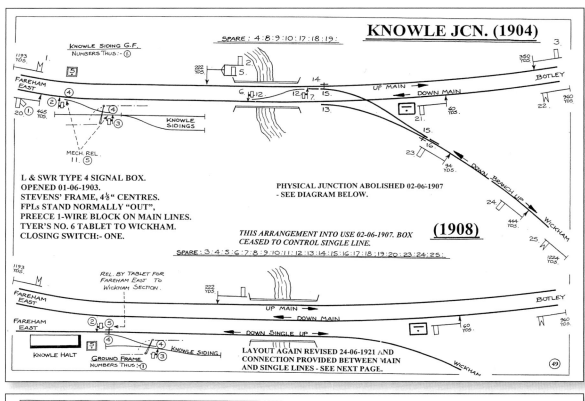

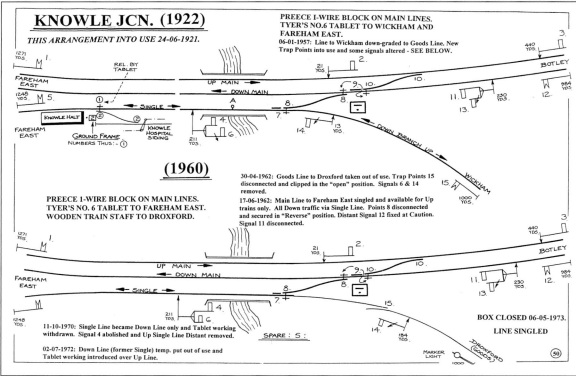

In the second plan (1904), the signal box has been moved to its more familiar position and for the present time the MV line feeds directly in to the Botley – Fareham route. By 1908 this arrangement had been altered, commensurate also with the building of the 'Fareham diversion'. The river bridge has also been widened to take the third line of rails. Note in both this and the previous example, the siding is worked by a separate ground frame.

Finally from 1921 a connection is provided allowing down Fareham trains to use the single line. A sketch of the track and signalling layout circa 1950 and which shows how access was possible for both Up and Down Meon Valley trains but Down trains only coming off the Botley (Eastleigh) to Fareham line. The distant signals likely became fixed shortly before WW1 as was the general policy of making such signals fixed both on single lines and also on the approach to a terminus. On this sketch the connections to the hospital siding are not shown.

Passengers and perhaps hospital staff at the tiny halt in BR days. Close examination will reveal the size of the name on the running-in board has altered.

The hospital siding, in use until closure on 30 April 1962, was on a slight 1 in 7,260 gradient and was served by Down goods trains only (see signalling diagrams). A crossover from the Down Botley to Fareham line was installed later allowing trains from Eastleigh to call at Knowle Halt as evidenced from a known signalling diagram of Knowle Junction box.

Following the closure of the Meon Valley line in February 1955, Knowle Halt was only served by trains on the Eastleigh to Fareham line. These trains then taking the old tunnel route to reach Fareham. Since its opening the stopping place had been known as "*Knowle Asylum Halt*", "*Knowle Platform*" and from 5 October 1942 simply "*Knowle Halt*".

The Halt did not always appear in public timetables and towards the end of its life trains only called there on hospital visiting days. Closure was announced for 12 August 1963 but having duly gone through the motions that day, it had to be hurriedly reopened when it was realised that a formal objection had been made. Final closure took place on 6 April 1964.

Fast forward to 2017 and given the transformation of the former hospital site (which closed in 1996) to housing known as Knowle Village, there is a strong case currently being made to reopen Knowle as a station once again.

Source References:

Public Record Office – LSWR Minute Books & BoT MT6 files

LSWR Working Timetable Appendix 1921

SR Working Timetable Appendix 1934

South Western Circle

County Asylum on-line records.

N15 No 30451 *Sir Lamorak* in charge of a long down freight at Knowle. This is a Salisbury – Brighton line freight, possibly travelling as far as Chichester where it will be reformed, it has certainly not come off the MV route and instead will have taken the facing connection on to the single line at Knowle Junction.

Tornado Time
And Not Referring to the Superb 60163

Living in Britain, and by that I include the areas of Wales, Scotland and Northern Ireland (fear not, what follows will have no political ramifications whatsoever – I am perfectly sure we all had more than enough of that towards the end of 2019), I suspect we are all guilty of conversations about the weather. 'Too hot…', '…too cold…', '… it was never like this years ago…', I could go on… . But occasionally some unusual weather occurrence can occur that really does warrant conversation and in consequence affects the railway; and be assured this is not '…the wrong type of snow' again either! Occasions we may recall so far as snow is concerned are the winters of 1927/8, 1947/8, and 1963, whilst 1975/6 are remembered for their heat and 1987 for the 'Great Storm'.

Between some of these dates came a fortunately rare occurrence in the form of a tornado that crossed parts of central and south-east England on the evening of 5 September 1958.

We were recently passed the official Southern Region report of the occasion and whilst containing no images it does give some indication of the effect to the railway of what was described as, "…a violent thunderstorm accompanied by torrential rain, the extreme conditions prevailed for some two and half hours". The consequence was '…earth slips, flooding, interrupted communication, electric defects on trains, and other obstructions especially widespread in the London East and London Central districts.' As is often the case with such extremes the area affected was fortunately limited and 'London West' escaped comparatively lightly; even so, for some time after, rail transport was severed along all the main lines in Kent.

The major incidents were detailed as follows:

So how do we illustrate an article on extreme weather that mainly occurred in the evening and overnight? Short answer, not easy, with perhaps the obvious response being to show the aftermath the next day. The problem is that even the next day – and days after – there does not appear to be anything recorded on film. (I would be delighted to be proved wrong…) As an alternative we are delighted to record some more of Graham Smith's excellent colour views courtesy of Richard Sissons, starting with this of 4 SUB unit No 5772 in January 1962. The location is not given but I am sure someone will enlighten us. Clearly there has not been much movement on the siding for a little time. In the period in question, the number '42' referred to a service on the route Charing Cross – Gillingham or Ramsgate via Parks Bridge and Sidcup.

Location(s)	Nature of incident	Lines affected	Date and time of clearance
Blackheath and Charlton	Earth slip	Down and Up	Sunday 7 September 6.30pm
Erith and Slade Green	Earth slip	Up	Monday 6 September 10.10am
Crayford and Bexley	Earth slip	Down and Up	Saturday 6 September 12.55am
Albany Park and Sidcup	Earth slip	Down Up	Saturday 6 September 8.0pm Saturday 6 September 8.50pm
Sevenoaks and Weald	Earth slips	Down and Up	Monday 8 September 4.00am
Bickley Junc. and Petts Wood Junc.	Earth slip	Down	Saturday 6 September Steam 8.30am. Elec. 12.45pm
St Mary Cray and Swanley	Earth slip	Down Up	Sunday 7 September 4.45pm Sunday 7 September 8.30am
Fawkham	Earth slip	Down and Up	Sunday 7 September 12.55am and speed limit imposed
Fawkham and Sole Street	Earth slip	Both	Saturday 6 September 8.20am
Otford and Bat & Ball	Earth slip at 11.25am 6-9-58	Down Up	Saturday 6 September 9.25am Sunday 7 September 5.30am
Bat & Ball and Sevenoaks	Earth slip	Down Up	Sunday 7 September 5.30am Sunday 7 September 5.30am
Clock House	Flooding	Both	Saturday 6 September 7.37am
Shoreham (Kent)	Falling chalk	Both	Saturday 6 September 1.55am
Greenhithe	Earth slips	Both	Saturday 6 September 4.30am
Gravesend Cntl.	Earth slip	Up	Saturday 6 September 1.00am
Blackheath and Kidbrook	Earth slip	Both	Saturday 6 September 4.55am
Woodside	Flooding	Both	Friday 5 September 11.41pm
Dunton Green and Polhill	Earth slip	Both	Saturday 6 September 5.00am
New Eltham and Albany Park	Earth slip	Both	Saturday 6 September 8.57pm
St Mary Cray station	Earth slip	Down Up	Sunday 7 September 4.45pm Sunday 7 September 8.30am
Dunton Green and Chevening Halt	Earth slip	Single	Thursday 11 September
East Grinstead and Ashurst Junc.	Earth slip	Single	Saturday 6 September 3.45pm 20mph speed restriction
Penshurst and Edenbridge	Earth slip	Up	SLW until 6.00pm Saturday 6 September. 20 mph speed restriction
Cowden and Edenbridge Town	Earth slip	Up	SLW until 4.50am Saturday 6 September
Morden Road Halt	Flooding	Single	Saturday 6 September 9.15am
Reigate and Redhill	Flooding	Both	Saturday 6 September 6.20am 35mph speed restriction
Forest Row and Hartfield	Earth slip	Single	Saturday 6 September 2.43pm
Horsted Keynes	Flooding	Both	Friday 5 September 10.17pm
Brockley and Honor Oak Park	Flooding	Down local	Saturday 6 September 3.00am
Purley and Kenley	Flooding at 3.20am 6-9-58	Both	5mph speed restriction
Dorking North	Flooding	All	Heavy delays, no actual blockage
Horley and Salfords	Fallen trees at 7.40pm and 11.15pm 5-9-58	Down local Up local Up local	Friday 5 September 8.45pm Friday 5 September 10.0pm Friday 5 September 12.10pm
Gomshall and Guildford	Earth slip	Both	Friday 5 September 11.30pm
Faygate and Crawley	Tree on line at 6.57pm	Both	Friday 5 September 8.10pm
Quarry Line	Falling chalk at 7.20pm	Both	Friday 5 September 8.48pm
Woldingham and Oxted	Earth slip	Down	5mph speed restriction
Caterham and Purley	Flooding at 7.37pm	Both	Friday 5 September 10.10pm
Hurst Green Junc. and Lingfield	Earth slip and broken culvert	Down	SLW until 7.0am 6 September. Temporary speed restriction of 10mph
Crowhurst Junc. North and Hurst Green Junc.	Defective culvert	Up	From 2.30pm 7 September

Move forward a few years to January 1987 and we see the car sheds at Orpington. One suspects it was not quite a normal service that day.

A personal favourite from this selection is this of Headcorn in April 1968. It almost makes one shiver looking at the scene. 'Proper colour' paintwork and signs although in the distance MAS is in use. We may also suspect visits to the wooden privy at the foot of the steps were as infrequent and rapid as possible.

On Saturday 6 September emergency services were operated in the London East district. Steam and diesel trains ran between coastal stations and Tonbridge or Chatham. Passengers were then transferred to available electric trains or used an emergency bus link. As lines were cleared so it was possible to operate some Hastings-Charing Cross trains via Redhill; the 3.26pm Ramsgate to London Bridge also ran via Redhill whilst the 8.35pm Victoria to Ramsgate worked via Sidcup.

There is a lovely quote when it comes to Cross Channel Services; 'Ostend services ran via Redhill or the Bexleyheath line'. We of course know what is meant but it still somehow conjures up visions of the actual ferry stopping at Platform 1! Things were slightly better explained when referring to 'Calais and Boulogne services were in the main diverted to and from Newhaven'. The Dunkerque (Night Ferry) service operated to and from Dover, the connecting train running via the Bexleyheath line.

By Monday 8 September, all routes were reopened to traffic with the exception of the Westerham branch. This should not be taken to infer the situation on the branch was especially challenging but instead it was a deliberate decision so that resources might be concentrated on the main lines. (The same report also made reference to what was then the regular flooding as occurred at Clock House at varying times during the evening and night of 16 July, Friday 5 September, and then later on Saturday/ Sunday 20/ 21 September.)

It also appears that not all locomotive crews were observing the imposed speed limits for on 26 September there is a note that the District Engineer, when making a personal inspection of the broken culvert between Hurst Green and Lingfield, observed the 1.47pm train from Tunbridge Wells West to Victoria pass over the restricted (10mph) length at 'a speed estimated to have been 30mph'.

Further reports categorised the difficulties in a specific area, the example below was from the District Traffic Superintendent at Orpington.

Sundridge Park	Earth slip on down line. In order 7.25am 6 September
Between Knockholt and Dunton Green	Earth slip
Sevenoaks	Earth slip
Between Sevenoaks and Tonbridge	Earth slip
Clock House	Flooding
Woodside	Flooding and earth slip
Maze Hill	Failure of track circuits
Charlton	Earth slip
Woolwich Dockyard	Flooding and earth slip
Woolwich Arsenal	Earth slip, up line
Abbey Wood and Plumstead	Flooding
Between Erith and Slade Green	Flooding, earth slip and trees fouling running lines
Slade Green	Failure of all track circuits
Dartford Junc.	Flooding of up line
Between Dartford and Stone Crossing	Earth slip
Gravesend Central	Earth slip
Greenhithe	Earth slip
Between Gravesend Cntrl. and Northfleet	Flooding
Blackheath	Flooding and earth slips
Between Welling and Bexleyheath	Flooding and earth slip
Bexleyheath	Earth slip
New Eltham	Flooding
Sidcup	Flooding and earth slip
Albany Park	Earth slip
Bexley	Flooding
Crayford	Earth slips
Bellingham	Flooding and earth slips
Between Bickley and Petts Wood	Flooding
St Mary Cray	Earth slip
Eynsford	Earth slips
Shoreham (Kent)	Three large trees obstructing running lines
Between Sevenoaks and Bat & Ball	Earth slip
Farningham Road	Instrument failure
Sole Street	Earth slips
Gillingham (Kent)	Flooding of up line
Beckenham Hill	Flooding

The report was signed by A Earle Edwards

At a stand at Sevenoaks on 13 January 1981. Presumably the driver (?) is at work with his paddle so it would appear as if a shoe has become dislodged.

London Central reported their specific difficulties in report rather than tabular form, some of the more interesting of these as:

"The storm dislocated most of the telephone communication throughout the district and great difficulty has been experienced in obtaining details of the resulting incidents; the information set out below comprises that which has so far been received and in some cases is sketchy.

Victoria – Gloucester Road Junction. At Victoria unit 4120 was defective resulting in the cancellation of the 8.0pm Victoria to Beckenham Junction and return 8.41pm Beckenham Junction to Victoria.

Track circuit failure occurred on the Up through line at Battersea Park from 7.49pm until 8.30pm.

At Thornton Heath, track circuit failures occurred affected the Up and Down through lines from 7.40pm until 9.5pm.

London Bridge – Brighton. The down local line between Brockley and Honor Oak Park was blocked from 8.30pm until 3.0am Saturday 6 September due to an earth slip.

At 8.18pm flooding of the down local line at Honor Oak Park was reported, this was cleared by 10.17pm.

The Down and Up Quarry lines between Coulsdon North and Earlswood were blocked at 7.20pm after the motorman of the 7.0pm Victoria to Brighton reported a fall of chalk. Traffic was diverted via Redhill until both lines were cleared at 9.48pm.

The Down and Up local lines between Horley and Salford were blocked from 7.40pm until 10.30pm and the Up line again from 11.15pm to 12.10am by trees falling on the line.

South Croydon to Tunbridge Wells West. Saunderstead signal box was struck by lightning and lost all communication at 7.14pm. Time interval working was adopted until 7.46pm when telephones were restored and used to maintain block working. Normal working from 11.20pm.

At 8.20pm an earth slip was reported on the Down line between Woldingham and Oxted and a 5mph speed limit imposed.

At 1.20am Saturday 6 September, it was reported that as a result of earth slips between Edenbridge Town and Cowden, single line working was in operation over the Down line between Edenbridge Town and Cowden. Normal working resumes 4.30am.

Headcorn again in April 1968. Any passengers are wisely contained within, but we may also note the chimneys are not smoking. So no fires or some other form of heating?

Hurst Green Junction to Haywards Heath. At 7.40pm there was no communication available between Hurst Green junction and Lingfield signal boxes and time interval working was adopted.

The Down line between Hurst Green Junction and Lingfield was blocked at about 8.00pm and single line working instituted over the Up line between Lingfield and Hurst Green Junction. The Down line was cleared at 7.10am Saturday 6 September and single line working was withdrawn with the 6.34am East Grinstead to London Bridge train.

Examination on the morning of Saturday 6 September revealed an earth slip between East Grinstead (Low Level) and St. Margarets Junction on the Up line demolishing East Grinstead South Up starting signal and shunt signal and St. Margarets Junction Up distant.

At Horsted Keynes both lines were flooded in the station and the current was isolated at 9.3pm. A taxi was provided to cover the train service until normal working was resumed at 10.17pm.

At 9.58am Saturday 6 September, three earth slips were discovered between West Hoathly and Horsted Keynes.

Tunbridge Wells West – Uckfield – Lewes. No signal box communication was available between Lewes Main Junction and Isfield from 8.10pm until 11.17pm and time interval working was adopted.

London Bridge – Arundel. Track circuit failures occurred at Tulse Hill affecting all lines at 9.00pm. Rectified at 9.22pm.

At 8.10pm flooding occurred at Dorking North resulting in heavy delays to trains until cleared at 9.47pm.

The 5.54pm Bognor Regis to Victoria was delayed by two minutes as a result of striking a branch of a tree between the Up distant and Up home signals at Ockley. The 6.52pm Horsham to Waterloo was cautioned and the branch was removed by the motorman of the 6.6pm Waterloo to Horsham.

West Coast. Storm water was reported above the sleepers at 6.5pm at Fishbourne Crossing and commenced subsiding at 6.25pm.

Mid-Sussex line. At 7.00pm the Up line between Faygate and Crawley was blocked as a result of trees being blown on to the up line. The line was cleared at 8.10pm.

Woodside-Selsdon. Flooding occurred between Bingham Road and Woodside at 9.0pm on the Down and Up lines.

The Up line was cleared at 11.41pm but the Down line remained blocked due to an earth slip. The Down line was cleared by Saturday morning start of work.

Three Bridges – Tunbridge Wells West. The single line between East Grinstead and Ashurst Junction is blocked by earth slips between East Grinstead and Forest Row and between Forest Row and Hartfield. A special bus service is operating between East Grinstead and Groombridge.

Norwood Junction – Sutton. At West Croydon a track circuit failure occurred affecting No 18/ 19 points (Goods to Up Main) from 7.45pm until 8.40pm.

The motorman of the 7.00pm Epson Downs to London Bridge requested that the train be taken out of service at Wallington as he was experiencing electrical shocks from the train. The matter was rectified by the motorman and the train was not withdrawn from service.

West Croydon to Wimbledon. At Mitcham the single line was blocked by flooding at 7.47pm and trains terminated at Mitcham from West Croydon, and at **Merton Park** from Wimbledon. It was not possible to obtain special buses. The line was cleared at 9.10pm.

At 6.30am Saturday 6 September, flooding of the single line was reported at Morden Road Halt and a shuttle service was introduced between West Croydon and Mitcham, the service between Wimbledon and Mitcham being suspended. The London Transport Executive were requested to allow rail passengers to use their ordinary road services. The line was cleared at 9.15pm.

Tattenham Corner and Caterham branches. At 7.15pm an earth slip was reported on the Down and Up lines between Kingswood and Chipstead, and a 5mph speed restriction was imposed which has since been lifted.

Both lines between Purley and Caterham were blocked shortly after 7.30pm owing to flooding and obstruction by debris. Passengers were diverted to ordinary bus services as it was not possible to obtain a special bus service. Both lines were cleared at 10.10pm but a 5mph speed restriction on both lines was imposed at 3.20am (Saturday) which has since been lifted.

Redhill – Tonbridge. At 11.10pm it was reported that both lines were blocked by an earth slip at Bough Beech between Edenbridge and Penshurst. The Down line was cleared at 4.45am (Saturday) and single line working is in operation over the Up line between Penshurst and Edenbridge.

At 4.44am it was reported that an earth slip had occurred between Penshurst and Lyghe Halt. Reported clear at 7.56am.

Redhill – Reading South. Both lines were blocked between Redhill and Reigate shortly after 7.00pm as a result of a subsidence under the Up line by Croydon Road underline bridge. Special buses operated between Redhill and Reigate and in connection with the next incident between Reigate and Gomshall. Both lines were cleared at 6.20am Saturday 6 September with a 10mph speed restriction on the Up line. Down trains being cautioned.

The Up line between Gomshall and Dorking Town was blocked shortly after 7.00pm as a result of a subsidence adjacent to Westcott Up intermediate and the line was cleared at 11.30pm. Passengers from the 7.50pm Reading South to Tonbridge which terminate at Gomshall were conveyed by special bus to Redhill (via Reigate)."

We conclude with the emergency arrangements that were put in place on the London (Eastern) District for boat trains the day following, Saturday 6 September:

Outward				
Booked from	**At**	**Actual working**		**Number of**
		From	**At**	**passengers**
Ostend				
Dover	10.30am	Dover	10.31am	297
	12.20pm	Dover	1.55pm	1,638
	4.50pm	Dover	6.6pm	662
	1.45am (Sun)	Dover	5.12am (Sun)	571
Boulogne				
Folkestone	11.20am			
Folkestone	6.40am	Newhaven	8.6pm	952
Dover	9.10pm	Newhaven	10.50pm	455
Calais				
Dover	1.5pm	Newhaven	4.48pm	580
Folkestone	4.10pm	Newhaven		

Shuttle services operated as follows:

London Bridge – Mottingham and Bexley to Dartford – until 9.0pm Saturday 6 September.
Also between:
Elmers End and Sanderstead
Elmers End and Addiscombe
Gillingham and Fawkham
Maidstone East and Swanley

Holborn Viaduct and Orpington via the Catford Loop. In all these cases no time of start and commencement is given.

As alternatives to the railway, a special bus service was provided between:

Orpington and Swanley
Mottingham and Bexley – until 9.0pm Saturday 6 September
Sevenoaks and Tonbridge
Sevenoaks and Otford
Swanley and Fawkham
Dunton Green and Westerham.

Finally in this sequence we see Headcorn again in January 1979. The train is Charing Cross – Ashford via Orpington (and vice-versa). It would also appear priority snow clearance has been given to the slow lines. Reverting back to the actual Tornado and the main subject of this article, the *West Sussex County Times* of 1958 revered in some detail to the extreme weather, speaking of record breaking hailstones, some between the size of a hen's egg and a cricket ball. Not surprisingly such an extreme of weather did considerable damage including dented cars, broken roof tiles and destroyed vegetation. Two oil storage tanks at the Isle of Grain were set on fire after being struck by lightning and there were numerous reports of electricity and telephone failure. Further detail is available at: https://www.netweather.tv/forum/topic/49236-the-horsham-tornado-and-hailstorm-5th-september-1958/

The electric services between Charing Cross and Cannon Street and Gillingham was augmented to assist in the clearance of passengers for Kent Coast services who transferred to and from steam services at Chatham. By 4.0pm all these passengers had been cleared, this clearance being assisted by passengers from Kent Coast stations circulating via Ashford and Hastings.

Through services via Reading and the Western Region ran normally except for delays caused by single line working between Penshurst and Edenbridge.

The following day an appeal was put out to the public not to travel unless absolutely necessary which allowed 32 steam trains between London and the Kent Coast to be cancelled. The actual details were 20 trains running via Chatham; nine Down and 11 Up, whilst 12 trains via Tonbridge, 2 Down and 10 Up, similarly did not run. The Up Tonbridge services included nine specials that had been scheduled for returning 'Hop-Pickers friends'.

If there was a light hearted moment, it was at the conclusion of the report when referring to the four delayed services that arrived at Victoria from Newhaven between 11.42pm and 2.36am compared with their scheduled arrivals from 9.42pm to 1.12am. The four trains carryied some 2,860 passengers. In addition to this a further 450 passengers arrived from Dover at 12.12am.

Many would of course have missed their onward connections although some 630 were quickly cleared by special buses to other London Termini – *630 less for the Southern to have to worry about!*

This left approximately 1,300 at Victoria where they slept on the actual trains or in the waiting rooms. To cater for this number the Victoria Refreshment Rooms were especially opened at midnight and remained as such until 6.00am. Tea trolleys were then used until 8.30am when the station cafeteria opened.

In the meanwhile a record was kept of the refreshments provided and it appears they were a hungry lot, for the total was:

1,600 sandwiches

700 cakes

140 pork pies

900 cups of tea

1 gallon of squash.

There was even praise for the service provided. I wonder if the same would apply should a similar situation arise 60+ years later?

As a finale we might mention that neither the *Railway Observer* nor the *Railway Magazine* appear to have commented on the events in their respective Autumn/Winter issues. This is slightly surprising as each had their 'spies' who would regularly report back and which in turn provide for such a fantastic source of information today. Perhaps the Southern were just so efficient that it was all over before there was time to note anything had happened. But then the Southern always did put their passengers first.

Southern 'Atmosphere'
Images From the Paul Hocquard Collection at The Transport Treasury

A pair of 'Charlies' at Guildford...

Railway Art comes in many forms. Perhaps the most obvious being a painting or poster, whilst others might also include decorative crockery, silver or glassware. Further along I personally might even say some signal box instruments are almost a work of art, the craftsmanship involved and polished brass to me a reminder of the skills of long forgotten craftsmen. ('Mrs' Editor does not quite agree with me on the latter point, and whilst she will tolerate a painting or model she did draw the line some years ago about having a tablet instrument in the lounge. I cannot see why.) Moving forward some could say an actual engine or item of rolling stock is similarly a work of art, especially perhaps those halcyon days recalling the products of the late Victorian and Edwardian era – again each to choice.

Another art form to me at least is the work of some especially talented photographers. Rod Hoyle is certainly in that league, as are George Heiron, Colin Gifford, etc, etc. These are also well known names but I would add one perhaps not so well known but to me equally talented, and that is Paul Hocquard.

Paul's material is now with the Transport Treasury and we are delighted to showcase some examples of his skills. No caption details or dates are available but then again I would suggest it is the picture itself which does the talking.

Removal of condemned stock, the dreaded 'hot-cross bun' symbol says it all.

Through the window...

Opposite: **Micheldever, late 1950s/early 1960s, before this the engine shown would have been in original condition.**

Bath Green Park and the station cat.

Opposite: **Midford signal box.**

Down 'Bournemouth Belle' at Waterloo.

Opposite: **Remember when trains carried mail and parcels…?**

Winter duty, Ashford.

Opposite: **Nine Elms and a rod for repair or replacement.**

'During the Small Hours'
A Tribute to H C Casserley
(With grateful thanks to Gerry Nichols and the SLS)

The year 2018 witnessed the passing of another railway stalwart, R M 'Richard' Casserley, son of the illustrious and previously deceased H C 'Henry' Casserley.

To many, Henry may have been the better known name and he was certainly the more prolific as regards books with something like seventy-five listed under his name when checking on that universal book store 'Amazon'.

Whilst Henry may have been the better known, we should not discount Richard whose own photographic output was also prolific and who for many years continued to make available both his and his father's images to all who sought help.

The photographic collection of both is now in the process of being broken up so whilst it will no longer be possible to obtain prints from 'a certain address in Berkhamsted' we can be certain that images attributable to both will continue to be seen for many years to come.

Reverting again to Casserley snr., whilst there probably are also few of us who do not have a Casserley book on our shelves, what is perhaps not so well known is that he also penned a number of short articles, some having been published and others not. The below was kindly passed to us by Gerry Nichols of the Stephenson Locomotive Society and makes for an interesting diversion during the time Henry lived alongside the Southern main line in South London.

"Those of us who are not privileged to reside alongside one or other of our main lines – an ambition cherished, no doubt, by most members of the Stephenson Locomotive Society – probably know little of what goes on during the dead of night, the hours when most mortals are asleep.

So another quandary, how to illustrate a piece on night trains originally written 90 years ago? Well a modern night scene was out of the question whilst scouring though the collections we have access to provided nothing really suitable and certainly nothing from that period. In the end we decided to choose two Casserley SR images, the first seen showing T9 4-4-0 No 710 alongside the original coaling stage at Nine Elms on 10 June 1926.

One might even venture the opinion that some of the lucky ones whose residences do overlook a railway line have no more than hazy notions as to what transpires at these times; preferring to remain in blissful un-consciousness of the possible types of trains or locomotives that pass which are normally not seen during the daylight hours.

As far as my own locality is concerned, the character of the line changes completely from its daytime aspect, and a few notes thereon will no doubt be of interest to some readers.

Night trains and night working have always held a fascination in my own case, stronger in many ways than that of the daytime. Unfortunately, on the Southern Railway there are no long-distance sleeping-car expresses, such as are to be found on the three trunk lines to the north, with all their romantic associations: 'Carlisle, Perth, Inverness'; what visions these names used to conjure in pre-Grouping days! Nevertheless, in its small way something of interest is to be found even on the Southern Railway; enough at any rate to cause me to rise from my bed (usually to the accompaniment of muffled domestic grumblings) and, armed with a spot light torch, stand shivering by the open window in a frequently successful endeavour to catch a severe chill. Shortly before 1am the last 'juice wagon' clatters its way down to Orpington and for the brief space of four hours we become a real railway once more.

Whilst traffic is naturally nothing like so heavy as during the daytime, there is quite a fair amount doing, particularly as regards goods trains, all of which are now scheduled during the night, owing to the congestion of so many superfluous electric trains during the daytime. These (the goods trains, of course) are hauled mainly by Wainwright 'C' class 0-6-0s, though occasionally an 'N' class 2-6-0 puts in an appearance, or more rarely still a Stirling 'O1' or a Brighton 0-6-0. At least one goods train is regularly 'King Arthur' hauled.

Engines running light to or from Ashford shops are frequently heard but seldom 'caught', owing to making their appearance at unexpected times. These are often a cause of much speculation.

Then there are the fast night trains, mainly conveying fish and newspapers, etc., but available in some cases for passengers also. The 3.5am from Victoria (public time 3am) to Tonbridge, Ashford and Dover is worked by a class 'L'. The 3.30am from Victoria to Sheerness (Faversham and Dover on Mondays only) is shown in the working book as being available for passengers, but does not appear in the public timetable!

For our second Casserley image we have moved to the opposite end of the Southern system with a Turnchapel train at Lucas Terrace Halt on 22 May 1925 in the charge of O2 No 207.

Until 1926 this train was usually hauled by a Stirling 'B1' 4-4-0 and a fine spectacle she made doing her 45mph or so up the 1 in 96, producing a miniature firework display. More recently, however, it has gone to the other end of the scale and is worked by a 'King Arthur', the engine presumably being changed at Gillingham. The 4am van train to Faversham and Ramsgate is another 'King Arthur' turn.

Most interesting of all, however, is the all-night local steam service between Holborn Viaduct and Orpington. It is intriguing to watch these trains plugging their way along, in charge of a Wainwright engine as they have for many years. The first of these is the 1.11am from Holborn Viaduct, worked by an 'H' class tank from Stewart's Lane, the engine returning with the 2.48am from Orpington. The 2.17am from Holborn is taken by a Bricklayer's Arms 'H' tank and this engine returns on the 3.53am from Orpington. There is also another up train, leaving Orpington at 3.47am and running via the Catford loop. This train is worked by a 'D' class 4-4-0 from Tonbridge, and is, incidentally, the only regular Tonbridge working remaining on the Chatham section.

Travelling by these night trains is also quite an interesting experience. The walk through the empty roads, save for an occasional policeman eyeing one's camera case suspiciously and the almost deserted stations, save for one or two sleepy-eyed porters and night workers. The train is comfortable and warm (steam-heated, of course) and that species of public nuisance, the fresh air fiend, who must have windows open, whatever the weather and temperature, is conspicuous by his absence.

A train I have on several occasions found very useful is the 3.1am, arriving at Holborn Viaduct at 3.41am. A tram leaves Gray's Inn Road terminus about 4 o'clock, in good time to catch the 4.25am from St. Pancras, for a full day's trip somewhere in the Midlands. At Herne Hill we find another steam night service train waiting, the 3.33am to Victoria and Sutton, in charge of an 'E5' 0-6-2T, a class not normally seen here during civilised hours. So, for a brief period one can, if so disposed, sample the flavour of the old Chatham Railway, as it used to be and for all its reputation it was not such a bad old line after all. Probably most members of the SLS, at any rate, would prefer the old order of things to the new. Shortly after 5 o'clock the too familiar clank clank is heard, and the first morning electric train – cold, cheerless and uninviting -bears its unfortunate early morning workers to town. The spell is broken, and we are living in the days of the Southern Railway once more."

Obituary, Alan Blackburn

Contributed by Mike King

Many readers of 'SW' will already be aware of the sad passing of Alan Blackburn in 2018. It is with gratitude we include these words from one who knew him well, Mike King.

Alan Blackburn, 1937-2019

Sadly, I have to report that Alan Blackburn – professional railwayman, preservationist, life-long modeller and contributor to these pages, passed away in a hospice in Woking on 8 May, after a short period of rapidly deteriorating health. He was 82.

Born on 4 January 1937, Alan grew up in various addresses in the Portsmouth area. His father died when he was just seven and he was befriended by a local signalman at Havant – while

I would not know what it was, but I know a man who would and that would have been Alan. (For the sake of completing the story we asked Mike King, who advised; "It is an ex-LBSCR 30ft covered carriage truck, SR No 4758 [ex-LBSCR no 128 of 1907] to Diagram 1164, photographed by Reg Lacy at Southampton Docks in 1938 - not long before withdrawal which took place in September of that year. Note another thing that Alan would almost certainly have commented upon - the odd wheelsets. Outer ones are Maunsell, centre set the original LBSCR 9-spoke pattern. All will be peculiar to Brighton stock, with 6ft 3in journal spacing, rendering them largely unusable elsewhere."

train watching adjacent to the signal box. This sowed the seeds for future career and interests. His first job at age 14 was with the railway at Fratton – in the signal box. National Service took him to Longmoor, where he was unimpressed by the way the Army ran their railway! This also sowed a seed in military history. Later a move to the Twickenham area saw him work in various signal boxes in the West London/Middlesex and Surrey areas. Seeing little future promotion in signalling, Alan moved to the permanent way offices at Croydon where he rose to become a senior member of the department and his knowledge of P. Way matters would be hard to beat. Indeed, his knowledge of all things railway was extensive and, once asked a sensible question, would give an authoritative answer in as much detail as one could wish for. Alan was also keen on walking and met Anka, his future wife, on a walking holiday in the Black Forest in 1967. They were married in 1969 and later made their home in Horsell, just north of Woking.

I first met Alan sometime in the late 1970s, but had seen his name against various articles on Southern wagons in the *Model Railway Constructor* since the mid-1960s. Indeed, at one point he was offered the job of editor of that magazine but, perhaps wisely, declined the offer. We were then commuters on the 07.29 Up and discussed all manner of railway subjects on the journeys to and from work. Just what fellow passengers thought of these conversations I know not since commuter trains are not renowned for chatter. The subject of wagons was probably the most discussed and I soon learnt that Alan, together with the late Ray Chorley, had produced the framework for a book on Southern Railway wagons, but doubted that any publisher would be interested. This was around 1971 and is before me as I write. It clearly demonstrates how much knowledge had already been amassed – long before others were remotely interested. A decade later in 1981 when I was approached by OPC to write a book on Southern wagons, I suggested to Alan that I could not attempt this on my own, but a joint effort might cover all the pre-Grouping Southern companies, with his and Ray's original synopsis dealing with the standard SR designs. Alan readily agreed and with the help of Gerry Bixley for the LBSCR, "An Illustrated History of Southern Wagons" was conceived (although it took many years and two different publishers for all four volumes to be completed). Alan contributed very much towards the more technical and historical aspects – drawing on his professional experience and contacts.

Alan also had a special interest in the railways of the Isle of Wight and at that time was chairman of the fledgling Isle of Wight Steam Railway – doing much in those early days to guide the organisation in the direction of becoming a successful preservation movement. He was also involved in carriage restoration on the Bluebell Railway. Time for modelling was also found – including producing some of the masters for several of Bob Wills' kits (now South Eastern Finecast) – and joining fellow members of The Model Railway Club in producing one of the pioneer P4 layouts – Bembridge. He was also their librarian. In more recent years he concentrated on 7mm scale but was also much interested in railways overseas. Family holidays often took them to various parts of Europe; Switzerland being a particular favourite and Alan always took an interest in the railways traversed.

Other railway projects in which he was much involved included the Speno rail-grinding train – which involved some night work and, after the October 1987 hurricane, surveying the track and tree damage to the railway from a helicopter hired from Fairoaks Airport. In the days immediately following the gale, it had proved impossible to travel anywhere on the railway system in the normal manner so this 'eye in the sky' was suggested by Alan – and readily agreed by BR management.

Since retirement, Alan set up meetings about railway history in his home for U3A – the University of the Third Age – which were well-attended and could always be relied upon for interesting discussion. More recently Alan suffered much back and knee pain, since which time he found mobility increasingly difficult. His last hurrah was just a few days before his passing; when he attended the opening of Kernow's new model shop in Guildford. With the aid of a wheelchair he visited, but was soon up and out of the chair, engaging all in conversation about, amongst many things, trackwork. Between 50 and 60 former colleagues from BR, the Isle of Wight Steam Railway, the Bluebell, the Model Railway Club, U3A and family attended his wake at the Railwayman's Sports Club in Woking on 29 May.

I learnt much from Alan – about many aspects of the railway – and also that railwaymen often see things with a different perspective to enthusiasts. A great deal of knowledge has gone with his passing. He is survived by his wife, two daughters and grandchildren, to whom we extend our condolences.

Mike King.

If as editor of SW I may add a few additional words; I personally came to know Alan in consequence of the shows I attended with my book stand for thirty years. Alan would approach in his own quiet way and carefully peer to see anything new that had been released on the Southern. He would never openly criticise another but I quickly came to realise if there was no purchase then there was something with which he disagreed – often as not I could not find out what! He was also an early and enthusiastic supporter of SW, contributing an article on weed-killing trains as well as several additions to 'Rebuilt'. He was much moved by the early passing of Graham Hatton and Tony Goodyear, agreeing to continue and complete Tony's 'History of the Southern Railway from Inception to Nationalisation' which appeared in eight parts. Alan's contributions, as with the others mentioned, will be sadly missed, as will a man who wanted things to be 'just right' – KJR.

The 'Croydon Tangle'

Jeremy Clarke

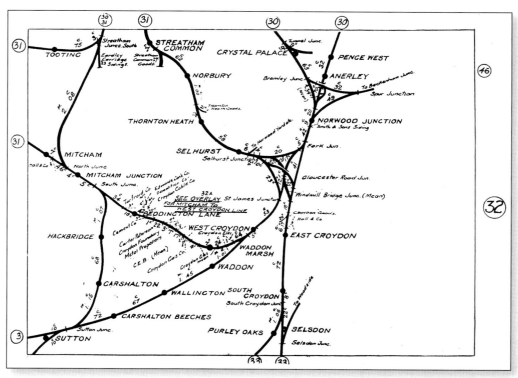

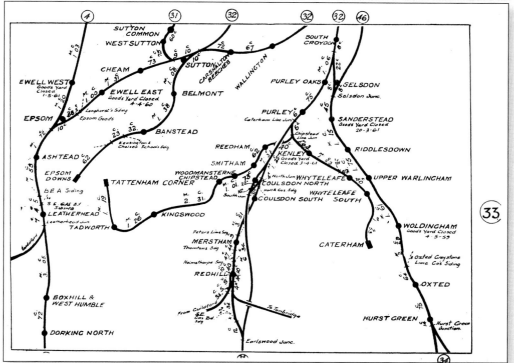

From the collection of the late Graham Smith was this fortunate find; part of a photocopied set of line diagrams covering the whole of the Southern Region albeit undated. Considering as Jeremy Clark puts it 'The Croydon Tangle', a location map is therefore essential.

The Railways of Croydon

Croydon came early on the railway scene and as befits its position ten miles south of central London the present railway infrastructure is thriving, if to the point its busiest line is now close to being overstretched even at off-peak times. There are seventeen stations in use in the Borough on no fewer than seven different routes. Three of the five former BR stations within the boundary, Waddon Marsh, Woodside and Bingham Road (now renamed Addiscombe), survive as stops on the Croydon Tramlink system.

From the passing of the London Government Act 1963 and its implementation on 1 April 1965, Croydon became one of the twenty 'Outer London' Boroughs created under the Act. Up to this time the town had had County Borough status; Coulsdon & Purley Urban District was added to it under the Act while some fringe wards were lost. The estimated population of the Borough in 2018 was a little over 385,000.

Apart from rail services centred on the town which run between Central London and much of suburban Surrey as well as out to the Sussex and Hampshire coasts, there have long been instances of 'through' traffic to/from points north of the Thames. The LNWR for example, and the LMS after it, for years worked a regular Willesden Junction-East Croydon service *via* the West London Railway, traffic later being restricted to parcels and perishable goods. For a very brief time the North Western also terminated at the unsuccessful Central Croydon station. This had only two short periods of use, closing for good in September 1890, the site being sold to the Council for a new Town Hall for the sum of £11,500. For an even shorter time the Great Eastern worked a Liverpool Street-Central Croydon via the Thames tunnel. Evidence of the site's former use may still be seen in the gardens adjoining the building.

The 'Sunny South Express', introduced in 1905 and jointly worked by the LBSCR and the LNWR, provided the principal long-distance 'through' passenger service between the South Coast resorts and the North-West of England. The immediate post-WW2 years saw a resumption of such traffic; the SR Timetable No 14 for summer 1953 for example shows return workings on Saturdays between Hastings and Brighton, and Birmingham New Street and Leicester London Road, calling at East Croydon. Indeed Manchester-Brighton services were still a feature well into the 1980s. An hourly service continues to operate on these lines starting/terminating at East Croydon though Milton Keynes Central forms the northern terminus nowadays.

Other developments include the 'Thameslink' service which, since 1988, has offered frequent direct cross-London trains going fifty miles out into Bedfordshire. The recently completed reconstruction of London Bridge and re-arrangement of the eastern approaches also permit a wider range of services to be provided, to Peterborough and Cambridge at present, perhaps with more to follow.

TfL's London Overground, opened in April 2010 and working out of West Croydon and through the Thames tunnel and Docklands into North London, is the closest the Borough has come to joining 'The Tube'. Past vague and sporadic aspirations include an extension of the Bakerloo Line down the Brighton Road from Elephant & Castle, as well as progression of the Victoria Line following much the same route south of Brixton, though neither is any nearer fruition than voiced suggestions and seems unlikely to be, for the foreseeable future anyway.

There is little railway development in the Borough's hilly south-eastern segment; that is, east of the Brighton main line, other than the northern ends of the Oxted route and the Caterham and Tattenham Corner branches. Transport connections within this area, particularly from the sprawling, primarily post-war, New Addington estate, with its population at the 2011 census in excess of 22,000, were relatively poor and were the principal reason for the introduction of the Tramlink system into its heart. This cut travel times into Central Croydon by half as well as much increasing capacity.

The earliest line within the town's boundaries, the Surrey Iron Railway (SIR), which opened on 26 July 1803, approached Croydon from the north-west, across Mitcham Common. The promoters, mainly owners of the forty or so factories and industrial developments along the lower reaches of the River Wandle, had proposed a canal to carry their goods to the Thames at Wandsworth, the Wandle itself not being navigable. But the eminent canal engineer, William Jessop, advised them that so much water would be removed from the river to feed it there would very probably be insufficient left to turn their mills. The SIR, to a gauge of 4'2", was the world's first public railway in the sense that anybody could use it to carry goods in their own vehicles if a toll were paid. To this day a publicly-evident smidgeon of its course is marked by 'Tramway Path' running eastwards from the Mitcham tram stop – now in the London Borough of Merton – and parallel to the Tramlink track for a distance of some four hundred yards.

The SIR terminated in Croydon at Pitlake, to the west of the present Town Centre and close to the point at which the eastern edge of the Wandle valley meets the rising ground on which much of Croydon stands. An extension under the title Croydon, Godstone & Merstham Railway (CG&M) opened on 24 July 1805 as part of a proposed scheme connecting Portsmouth to the capital. (It never got to Godstone, finishing at the works of the Greystone Lime Company at Merstham.) A strongly-supported – vocally anyway! – proposed canal rivalled the line, both being designed to permit avoidance of the perils of French naval intervention in the transport particularly of military personnel and gear in the Channel and around the Isle of Thanet. But the victory at Trafalgar on 21 October 1805 negated the need for such a link. The difficulty the CG&M had had in raising capital to meet its ultimate aim mirrored the inability of the canal proposal to do likewise.

Traffic ceased on the SIR on 31 August 1846 by which time an extension of the London & Croydon Railway to Epsom had been authorised, the company having merged on 27 July that year with the London & Brighton and others to form the London, Brighton & South Coast Railway. Closure of the Surrey Iron Railway followed a period of wrangling between the London & Croydon, the London & Brighton and the London & South Western and the SIR itself, which included various

Stone blocks and rail from the Surrey Iron Railway.

proposals for upgrading the latter and connecting it to the LSWR main line at Earlsfield. The company was finally wound up in August 1848.

The mainly single track line between West Croydon and Wimbledon, which Tramlink now uses, follows the route of the SIR south of Merton, other than a deviation on the approach to the Croydon terminus. It opened on 22 October 1855. (The section of the SIR north of Merton followed the River Wandle to Wandsworth.) The Brighton leased the line in 1856 and purchased it two years later. Electrification came on 6 July 1930, closure for incorporation into Tramlink following on 2 June 1997, though the last train had run three days earlier. Trams began running over it on 29 May 2000. Only Waddon Marsh, which opened with electrification, was in the Borough.

The second line to appear was built by the London & Croydon Railway (L&CR), engineered by William Cubitt. The terminus was on the London Road at the northern end of the town, occupying much of the terminal basin constructed by the Croydon Canal. After many vicissitudes this had opened on 22 October 1809 to coincide with the completion of the Grand Surrey Canal that provided it with access to the Thames by a junction at New Cross. The canal had never been financially successful and there was perhaps some relief among shareholders when the Railway proposed to purchase it as the basis for its route to the Capital. That relief may have been tempered by the fact they – the proprietors – were asking a price of £40,000 for the canal as a navigation rather than the railway's proposition to pay a lesser amount for it as a collection of assets. The proprietors' own figure was, nevertheless, only a quarter of the nominal capital value. The railway company sought arbitration for satisfaction but didn't get it. The arbitrator agreed with the canal shareholders and fixed the value at £40,250. In addition he awarded them the princely sum of one shilling (5p) in respect of lost profits.

It may be noted that recent housing development along the eastern fringe of what remains of the Down side marshalling yard south of Norwood Junction, which occupied much of the former Croydon Common, is fronted by Canal Walk and Towpath Way. These lie on the exact line of the canal in this vicinity as indeed does the length of track between Spurgeon's Bridge, north of west Croydon, and Gloucester Road. The adjoining footpath here is the original towpath, the track being in the former channel. Three other portions survive, South Norwood lake locally, formerly one of the two reservoirs, and beyond the Borough a small, rather 'beautified' part of the channel in Betts Park in Anerley – in a rather sorry state at last viewing! – and a curved pond at Dacres Wood at Forest Hill.

As was quite common in canal acts of the time, the Croydon Canal was empowered to build short 'railways', and in this instance specifically to construct one joining its basin in London Road to the SIR at Pitlake. It is uncertain exactly when this tramway was laid down but soon after the canal's opening it is reported '... [this] *has increased the business of the canal*'. The tramway was taken up shortly after the purchase of the canal by the L&CR though its route is represented by Tamworth Road which falls into the Wandle valley with the line from West Croydon to Sutton and Epsom in its shadow. It now carries part of Tramlink's Croydon town centre circular one-way on-street section.

The London & Croydon Railway opened on 5 June 1839,

four years to the day since incorporation. From its position in what had been the canal basin it went north to make a junction with the London & Greenwich Railway at Corbett's Lane, whence it had running powers on payment of tolls for the last 1¾ miles into London Bridge station. Clearly much of the canal route with its twists and turns to maintain a level channel proved unsuitable for direct and easy adaptation to railway purposes, particularly where it then had to drop through twenty-six locks down the face of the clay ridge that encircles south London. Perhaps for that reason – in part anyway, for railway cost estimates at the time always seemed wildly optimistic – the Croydon's ultimate price worked out at all but three-and-a-half times the estimate of £185,000. A proportion of this centred around additional land purchases; the angle required to maintain the stability of the clay in the sides of the deep cutting down to New Cross had been seriously underestimated.

Apart from West Croydon – the prefix belatedly dating from April 1851, nearly five years after amalgamation with the London & Brighton which had its own Croydon station, later classified with several variations, 'East' – only Norwood Junction on this route, eight miles and fifty-five chains from London Bridge, is within the Borough. The boundary with the adjacent London Borough of Bromley lies forty-eight chains to the north of it, at the bridge carrying the Crystal Palace-Beckenham Junction line over the ex-L&CR route.

The remains of an atmospheric pipe from the London and Croydon line.

The extension of the London & Croydon to Epsom opened on 10 May 1847. This had been preferred by Parliament over an independent route to the town supported by the London & South Western from a junction at Surbiton. That had to wait another twelve years, the junction then being at Raynes Park. The preference was due to the rather greater populace the London & Croydon would serve and the anticipated speed of the trains powered by the Clegg & Samuda atmospheric system the company had on trial when the line was proposed, a system much favoured by Cubitt. By the time construction had been completed however the atmospheric system had proved a costly failure, the last train running a week beforehand. The only part of the L&CR line to be worked in this way lay between Croydon and Forest Hill though testing had taken place as far north as New Cross.

Because of the difficulty presented by the atmospheric pipe at crossovers and pointwork, a new bi-directional track exclusively for use by atmospheric trains had been laid on the down side between New Cross and Norwood Junction by November 1845. But to reach the L&CR terminus it had to cross the London & Brighton line, that is from the east side of the layout to the west. This was achieved by construction of a flyover south of Norwood Junction, probably the first in the world. Following abandonment of the system in May 1847, this line became a Down slow, augmented in 1854 by another line on the Up side. To this day the four tracks north of Norwood Fork Junction are paired by direction rather than by use, the 'fast' lines being in the centre of the formation. The approaches to the wrought iron girders of the flyover itself were of timber trestle construction, though in time embankments superseded them. Natural deterioration of the wrought iron saw steel girders erected in their place. The majestic Norwood Fork Junction signal box, on its tall brick locking room that enabled the signalman to look down on the span, lay tucked into the tight space between the Down main line and the bridge's supporting piers. It was overlooked by a tall signal post carrying three dolls, one for each of the accessible routes, with original Brighton lower quadrant stop and distant signals. Seeing any of the latter three 'clear' was rare.

The extension to Epsom required rebuilding of West Croydon station, which stands almost 10½ miles from London Bridge, on a rather more angular NNE/SSW axis than the original. At a further reconstruction made under SR auspices in 1932/3, a new station building appeared at the Down end facing London Road. A short bay was let into the south end of the Up platform to accommodate Wimbledon line trains. Incidentally, in the course of this renovation several atmospheric pipes were unearthed. The original L&CR building in Station Road survives in use as a motor spares outlet but in 2012 a new entrance opened near to it conveniently closer to the bus station and tram stop than the SR one.

Half-a-mile south of the station the Wimbledon line, which ran independently of that to Epsom, curved sharply away to take up its north-westerly direction towards Mitcham. Nowadays the Tramlink track is carried to the alignment on a reversible, single-track flyover at Reeves Corner to/from its looped on-street

section in Church Street and Tamworth Road. The only other station on the Epsom line in the Borough is Waddon, 11½ miles from London Bridge and, being in the Wandle valley, is set no less than thirty feet lower than West Croydon. The boundary with the London Borough of Sutton is only a quarter-mile further on.

A non-electrified freight line paralleled the Wimbledon route for more than two miles beyond West Croydon to serve a number of important and well-established industrial developments extant in the Wandle valley. It opened in May 1930 as a passing place because the regular and more frequent 20-minute headway electric service to Wimbledon due to begin two months later would have restricted the paths available for the quite heavy freight movements created by those industries. Much of this line beyond Waddon Marsh Halt was effectively formed by joining up several existing industrial sidings already in place. For that reason the section beyond Waddon Marsh was then treated as a long siding.

Croydon gasworks opened in 1867 on the Down side immediately at the point the line straightened to head north-west; the first of two power stations followed in 1896, this on the Up side. These installations were also in time rail connected and with enough siding accommodation to require their own shunting engines. An almost continuous flow of coal to feed these utilities was worked over the former atmospheric line flyover from Norwood Junction's down marshalling yard in trainloads generally of between thirty and thirty-five wagons. Norwood's fleet of ex-LBSCR 'C2X' class 0-6-0 and 0-6-2T 'radial' tank engines – the usual motive power until the later 1950s – often found difficulty taking more up the ⅜-mile at 1 in 49 to the flyover, particularly given the two speed-restricted crossovers that led to its foot. (I never saw one stall but some came mightily close to it!) Neither the Waddon Marsh freight line nor the utility works survive other than the two massive chimneys of Croydon 'B' power station planned in the mid-1930s but, due to suspension of construction in wartime, not completed until 1950. This was established on the down side north of Waddon Marsh Halt, the chimneys now standing in splendid, if rather sad, isolation beside an Ikea superstore in the retail park now occupying the site with the Ampere Way tram-stop, an obvious reference to the site's former use, which serves it.

As noted earlier the London & Croydon and the London & Brighton (L&B) amalgamated with others in 1846 to form the LBSCR. The L&B had had running powers over Croydon tracks north of Norwood Fork Junction where the two converged, ⅜-mile south of Norwood Junction station. Similar tolled running powers were in force for the London & Brighton over the London & Greenwich from Corbett's Lane Junction. The L&BR opened from Norwood Fork to Haywards Heath on 12 July 1841, the extension to Brighton following on 21 September. Stations on that line within the Borough are East Croydon, South Croydon, Purley Oaks, Purley and Coulsdon South. Only the first and penultimate stations of those five opened at the time, the latter as Godstone Road. It had a short first life, closing on 1 October 1847 because of poor patronage. Stoats Nest (Coulsdon) had also opened with the line about a mile further south of Purley but it also had a relatively short life, of only fifteen years.

South Croydon was established on 1 September 1865 as the southern terminus of an extension of track from the Brighton's independent New Croydon station, which opened on 1 May 1862 on the west side of East Croydon. This arose from the South Eastern's presence here, in the main the result of Parliamentary interference – nothing new there then! Essentially the route belonged to the Brighton. But while the London & Brighton Bill was being considered in 1837, someone on the Parliamentary Committee must have looked at a map and pointed out that if the route as presented were to go forward there would be two routes running more or less parallel for the seven miles between Penge, where the South Eastern route to Dover was to begin, and Purley, where it turned away south-eastwards to climb the dip slope of the North Downs above the Caterham Valley. Government thus rescinded its 1836 authorisation of the SER line in the belief there would never be enough traffic to justify such an arrangement. Instead the company was instructed to share the Brighton line as far as 'north of Earlswood Common', that being deemed a convenient point for it to turn east towards Dover. Naturally, both parties objected most strongly to the proposed arrangement but Parliament would not be moved though it took some inducements to be offered to both, but especially to the South Eastern, including authority to purchase the whole of the shared 11½ miles, before reluctant agreement was reached. That point 'north of Earlswood Common' is nowadays known of course as Redhill, a product of the railway age as there was nothing here before the Brighton Line arrived. (The name Redhill emanates from the Fullers Earth that has been mined for centuries from an outcrop of the underlying Greensand. The high iron content gives it a rusty red colour, hence Red Hill.) The two companies had separate stations here at first, both known as Reigate, that town being the nearest and about 1½ miles to the west. The Brighton laid out its station south of the junction until the SER rebuilt its own on the present site for joint use and opened it in May 1844. The LBSCR station became the expansive, well-equipped goods yard. (The SER had its own Redhill yard tucked into the curve of the Dover route taking up its easterly direction.)

The South Eastern had paid the Brighton half the estimated construction cost of the shared 11½ miles when, even before it had been completed, Parliament suspended the order to share. Instead it decided the Brighton would retain ownership of the 5¾ miles between Norwood and Coulsdon, the SER taking over ownership of the remaining 5¾ miles to Redhill, obviously with reciprocal running powers. It could never be a satisfactory arrangement for either party, leaving the Brighton incensed at the loss of the more expensive half of the route with its great chalk cuttings and mile-long tunnel under Merstham for half the overall cost, but more particularly by loss of control of the junction at Redhill. This caused considerable friction between the two, right up until Grouping in 1923; and though matters were improved following opening of the SER's 1868 main line through Sevenoaks, the arguments continued. Both companies regularly made representations to the Railway Commissioners, the Brighton contending the South Eastern gave its own traffic priority, the SER saying the Brighton dominated the available 'paths'.

The two companies being represented at East Croydon, they were obliged by the Parliamentary order to charge equal fares thence to London Bridge. But the Brighton, perhaps smarting from the SER's constant sniping, opened New Croydon on 1 May 1862 for the exclusive use of its local services. It took the form of a simple island platform on the up side at East Croydon though segregated from it by sidings and a fence and served by a separate booking office. It was reached by a new double-track line from a junction at Gloucester Road on the route to West Croydon. The Brighton then contended that by this separation and a different station name it could legitimately charge a different, more competitive – cheaper! – fare than at the 'shared' station. Extension to South Croydon was undertaken a little more than three years later as New Croydon had proved to be an inconvenient terminus.

Godstone Road station re-opened in August 1856 as Caterham Junction concurrently with the independently promoted branch to Caterham, but only after the South Eastern, which worked the branch from the first on the Caterham company's behalf, sued the LBSCR to force the reopening. The SER was in possession here because of an agreement between it and the Brighton made in 1849 that the area east of the Brighton Line and north of the SER's main line into Kent from Redhill should be considered SER 'territory'. On that basis the SER objected to the Brighton 'lending' rolling stock to the Caterham company when it began operation. The Brighton had insisted the layout at the junction provide no direct connection with the main line but then proved very obstructive to Caterham passengers, and especially following the Caterham Railway's bankruptcy in 1859 and the SER's subsequent takeover. Among other obstacles the LBSCR refused 'through' booking but then provided little time for tickets to be purchased

London, Brighton & South Coast Railway.

D. 671.

£10 REWARD.

WHEREAS, at about Two o'clock on the afternoon of Thursday, the 12th January, 1888, some evil-disposed person or persons did wilfully and maliciously tamper with the Norwood Spur Junction Distant Signal, by placing a large stone under the lever, so as to prevent its working, thereby seriously endangering the safety of the traffic,

The Directors hereby give notice that the above Reward of Ten Pounds will be paid to anyone who shall give such information as will lead to the conviction of the offender or offenders.

(By Order)   **A. SARLE,**
LONDON BRIDGE TERMINUS,   *Secretary & General Manager.*
January, 1888.

(1,000)   Waterlow and Sons Limited, Printers, London Wall, London.

before the connecting services departed. It would appear that in some instances the booking offices remained defiantly closed and on occasions passengers who had managed to purchase tickets were forcibly detained to prevent their making connections. Despite appeals to the Railway Commissioners and a lawsuit that prompted a 'Leader' in The Times condemning Brighton attitudes, this interference was not finally eradicated until the station and its layout were rebuilt during the line's quadrupling between 1896 and 1899, direct junctions then being put in though time may have tempered the practices as the two companies generally became more co-operative.

The Purley name had come into use on 1 October 1888. Kenley, 1¼ miles from Purley, is the only station on the Caterham branch within the Croydon boundary, the line passing into Tandridge District shortly before Whyteleafe station, a near-1½ miles further on.

The first part of the route to Victoria from Crystal Palace (completed in stages by 1 October 1860) had opened on 1 December 1856, the spurs to/from Norwood North Junction to join it at Crystal Palace coming into use ten months later. But the gradients and curvature of much of the line as well as its meandering course made it unsuitable for 'fast' traffic. The Brighton opened a cut off on 1 December 1862 from Windmill Bridge Junction, a half-mile north of East Croydon, to join that line at Balham. (The Norwood Fork-Selhurst spurs opened at the same time.) This line followed much of a proposed and authorised earlier route that had come to nothing. Though only 1¼ miles were lopped off the journey, this line's rather easier gradients and directness saved considerable time. Stations in the borough are Thornton Heath, which opened with the line, Selhurst (1 May 1865), and Norbury, this also a later addition, not appearing until January 1878 to promote speculative housing development. The boundary with Lambeth is only a quarter-mile or so north of Norbury station. As befitted the rising status of the West End, quadrupling of the line took place between 1900 and 1903, mainly on the east (Down) side, the stations all being rebuilt in red brick in contemporary style.

In what might be termed something of a reversal, the line south of South Croydon had already been quadrupled, this arising from the Brighton's continuing feud with the South Eastern over Redhill junction. In 1882 the SER had sought use of the former London & Croydon Up local line from Corbett's Lane Junction into London Bridge. The Brighton protested, citing its sole use for more than thirty years and contending the volume of its traffic far outweighed that of the South Eastern. In this the Brighton had right on its side because the South Eastern, counteracting the 12-mile long distance advantage to Dover of the LCDR, had opened the new main line between St Johns and Tonbridge via Sevenoaks throughout in 1868 (see SW21). As a result its original route via Redhill had become a secondary one, though the company still used it, particularly for freight traffic so as to realise optimum line occupation over the heavy gradients through the Downs. Nevertheless, in 1883 the SER put in the necessary connection at Corbett's Lane. But at the same time, in further

retaliation, the company removed some connections the Brighton had laid in at London Bridge in 1878 to improve operational flexibility. (The South Eastern had taken a 999-year lease on the London & Greenwich on 1 January 1845; it was still independent at Grouping in 1923.) The Brighton appealed to the Court of Chancery but lost.

Discussions to settle things dragged on without resolution until arbitration was sought, the matter being referred to Sir Henry Oakley, general manager of the Great Northern. He found in the SER's favour in July 1889, stipulating the Brighton's annual fee for use of the L&GR's lines into London Bridge should rise from £14,000 to £20,000. The LBSCR's Chairman, Samuel Laing, later told shareholders he thought the settlement cheaply bought. Parliament approved the arrangement in 1890.

But this did nothing to settle the continuing problem of what the Brighton considered unwarranted obstruction of its traffic by the SER on the still double-track line north of Redhill, where the South Eastern continued to take full advantage of its control of the junction. Biting the bullet, in 1894 the Brighton secured powers for widening. There was little opposition, the South Eastern, which still considered the Brighton unfairly exercised a near-monopoly of available paths – which it did because it had no other route! – naturally being in favour. The new lines went in on the west side from South Croydon, rejoining the original route just north of Earlswood and south of – and so avoiding! – Redhill, a distance of seven miles. The line opened on 5 November 1899 though only for goods traffic south of Stoats Nest until 1 April 1900 when passenger services commenced throughout. Purley Oaks and Stoats Nest & Cane Hill stations were opened with the new line, the former about midway between South Croydon and Purley, the latter ten chains north of the boundary between the two companies. This was at about the site of the original Stoat's Nest, which had closed in 1856 with the re-opening of Godstone Road/Caterham Junction. Crossovers between 'old' and 'new' lines for Brighton use were installed here too.

This new route, being without stations between Coulsdon and Earlswood, naturally carried most of the company's fast services. It was named 'The Quarry Line' because of its deep chalk cuttings and 1¼-mile long 'Quarry' tunnel through The Downs. Stoats Nest – eventually Coulsdon North after several permutations – besides serving the new route was laid out to form the outer-suburban terminus in place of South Croydon. As such, the final section of the Brighton's war-delayed suburban 6,700v overhead electrification programme reached it in April 1925, though by then the decision had been taken by the management of the new Southern Railway to adopt the ex-LSWR 660v third rail system. The six-mile long section between Windmill Bridge Junction and Coulsdon North was among the last to be re-equipped, overhead elimination finally coming in September 1929.

The loco depot for engines working the local services which had opened at Coulsdon North in 1900 lost its raison d'être with electrification and closed in 1928, at the same time as the South Eastern's small but up-to-date 1898-built depot at Purley.

Purley engine shed, built by the SECR in 1898. Legend has it that post-electrification it was used to stable the Royal train when such service was required for the Derby meeting. It closed as an engine shed in 1928 but remains in (unspecified) railway use.

From Coulsdon the Quarry line stays on the west side of the original for about 1½ miles before crossing over it at Star Lane and continuing on the east side to Earlswood. (The boundary between SER and LBSCR property is actually ½-mile south of Redhill Junction, hence the vagueness of 'north of Earlswood Common'. Extension of the four tracks to Balcombe tunnel had been completed in stages by 1910.)

In 1885 H Cosmo Bonsor had purchased Kingswood Warren, near the head of the Chipstead Valley, which winds from Coulsdon up to the heights of Epsom Downs. As a resident and with his presence on the Board of the South Eastern as well as holding other influential positions, Bonsor was instrumental in having the company build the Chipstead Valley Railway, the first part opening – to Kingswood (surprise-surprise) – in November 1897; that same year Bonsor was elected as the company's Chairman. The Brighton, being in possession at the point in Coulsdon at which the valley opens, the SER started the line from a junction on the Caterham branch at Purley. It plunges down and burrows beneath the main lines and then runs closely parallel to them for a mile before turning sharply westward into the valley on a fifteen-chain radius curve. Smitham station is on this curve and underwent reconstruction in 2006 when the main A23 Brighton Road was diverted from the centre of Coulsdon to pass beneath it. A public vote saw the name changed to Coulsdon Town from May 2011.

The branch rises continuously from the bridge under the Brighton line with nearly three miles at 1 in 80 as it nears its summit just north of Tadworth. Extension from Kingswood 'for Burgh Heath' to Tattenham Corner occurred in two stages, completed in June 1901, the final 1¼ miles falling at 1 in 100

until a few chains short of the station, which is 495' above sea level, (cf West Croydon at 175'). Two short tunnels were required in the section between Kingswood and Tadworth, the 310 yards of Kingswood tunnel and the minute Hoppity tunnel (bridge), of just 37 yards. Until electrification Tattenham Corner generally saw traffic only on race days, trains usually reversing at Tadworth. Stations within the Borough are Reedham, Coulsdon Town (the former Smitham) and Woodmansterne. All three were opened in the 20th century, the simple single-island Woodmansterne, just over a quarter-mile short of the boundary with Reigate & Banstead District, as late as 1932 to serve new inter-war housing.

Whilst with the South Eastern, the extensions into the Croydon area of the Mid-Kent Railway, opened from Lewisham to Beckenham in January 1857 and worked by the SER, must be mentioned. Addiscombe was reached from New Beckenham in April 1864, and the Selsdon line opened by the SER and the Brighton jointly from a junction at Woodside in August 1885. That line closed to all local passenger traffic for the duration of the war by March 1917 though some through trains – passenger and freight – continued to use it. Oxted line traffic was withdrawn from Selsdon in January that year but re-instated in March 1919; Oxted trains ceased to call from June 1959 though some evidence of the platforms remain. Stations between Woodside and Selsdon did not reopen until electrification in September 1935. Only Woodside and those stations south of it were in the Borough, the next one north, Elmers End, being just on the wrong side of the boundary, in Bromley; Woodside itself opened in July 1871, mainly because of its proximity to Croydon racecourse.

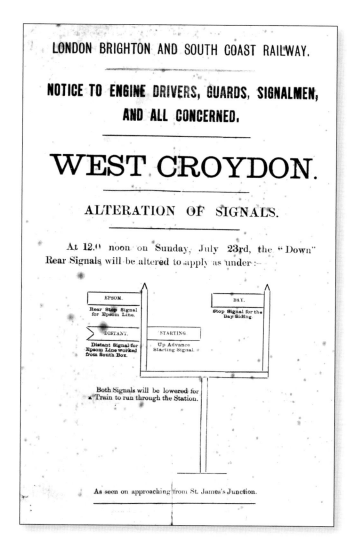

LONDON BRIGHTON AND SOUTH COAST RAILWAY.

NOTICE TO ENGINE DRIVERS, GUARDS, SIGNALMEN, AND ALL CONCERNED.

WEST CROYDON.

ALTERATION OF SIGNALS.

At 12.0 noon on Sunday, July 23rd, the "Down" Rear Signals will be altered to apply as under :—

EPSOM.
Rear Stop Signal for Epsom Line.

BAY.
Stop Signal for the Bay Siding.

DISTANT.
Distant Signal for Epsom Line worked from South Box.

STARTING.
Up Advance Starting Signal.

Both Signals will be lowered for Train to run through the Station.

As seen on approaching from St. James's Junction.

Selsdon line stations had a chequered career. Bingham Road opened with a 'Halt' suffix in September 1906, the station being rebuilt and the suffix dropped at electrification. Coombe Road opened with the line, at first as Coombe Lane Halt, the change again coinciding with installation of the third rail. Selsdon also opened with the line but as Selsdon Road, a much more accurate noting of its location vis-à-vis Selsdon itself, all but two miles from and nearly 300' higher than the station. The line itself went in May 1983 and Elmers End to Addiscombe closed in June 1997. Much of the mileage has been incorporated into Croydon Tramlink whose Addiscombe stop sits in the 'V' formed by Bingham Road's junction with Addiscombe Road. Both of these were bridged by the railway but the spans and the approach embankments on both sides were removed to bring the tram tracks down to road level.

Now that Selsdon has appeared, the northern end of the Oxted line is to be considered. This route, or one closely resembling it, had first been proposed in 1864 by a pseudo-independent company, very probably with backing from some LBSCR directors including its Chairman, Leo Schuster. Its Bill was withdrawn however with the agreement of the Brighton, as was a rival SER one for a line from Croydon to Eastbourne. (One

assumes this was proposed to start at or close to Addiscombe.) But the Surrey & Sussex Junction Railway company remained in being and the following year had a Bill passed for a line between Croydon and Tunbridge Wells on much the same route as the earlier one. The Brighton was to work it. The SER objected to this on the grounds it contravened the 1849 agreement that neither would encroach on the other's 'territory'. The Brighton countered by pointing out that the proposal did not so contravene as the line was to connect Croydon with Groombridge, both already on its system. It further contended that both Houses of Parliament had taken that agreement into consideration before passing the Bill. The counter may have been considered by Parliament as within the letter of the 1849 agreement but the proposals certainly contravened the spirit.

By way of retaliation, in 1865 the South Eastern, astonishingly, joined forces with its great Kentish rival, the London, Chatham & Dover Railway, to present a Bill for a London, Lewes & Brighton Railway (LL&BR) starting from Beckenham. Such were the disputes between the companies concerning the S&SJR as well as challenges regarding the legitimacy of some land purchases that arbitration was called for. The arbitrator, the Duke of Richmond, found in the Brighton's favour in March 1869, awarding the company £500,000 and the S&SJR then being transferred to its ownership, something the Brighton had not foreseen. But thereby it was required to complete the railway against a penalty of £50 per day. But this was a very difficult financial period for railways in general, mainly brought about by the collapse of the bankers Overend & Gurney in May 1866, and seeing there was little hope of gaining any profit from the line the Brighton sought to abandon the project in the Parliamentary session of 1870. Disappointingly, permission was refused. The company then took the decision to abandon those works that had been completed and pay the maximum limit of the penalty of £32,250 imposed by the Bill. (No doubt with some relief at removal of the S&SJR threat, the Joint LL&BR Bill was withdrawn.)

In the later, rather more co-operative climate, the Brighton and the South Eastern agreed to resurrect and finish the works though another Bill was required to alter the connections at the southern end which, rather than making a junction at Groombridge, would now meet and make an end-on junction at East Grinstead with the line building from Lewes via Culver Junction. However, joint working would be undertaken from South Croydon to Crowhurst, where the SER's original Redhill-Tonbridge line crossed its path, while the remainder southward would be solely Brighton-owned. A double-track north-to-east spur at Crowhurst would permit the South Eastern to gain their former main line. The Crowhurst Spur and the Croydon, Oxted & East Grinstead Railway opened throughout on 10 March 1884; the line from Lewes to East Grinstead had been commissioned nearly eighteen months previously. (The northern part of this is now, of course, the Bluebell Railway.) Stations in the Borough on this line were at Selsdon, and still are at Sanderstead, which opened with the line, and Riddlesdown, provided by the Southern in June 1927. The line passes into Tandridge District shortly before reaching Upper Warlingham, almost two miles further on. (See SW46.)

LONDON BRIGHTON AND SOUTH COAST RAILWAY.

Notice to the Officers and Servants of the
London Brighton and South Coast and South Eastern Railways.

PURLEY STATION.

Opening at 12.0 noon, on Sunday, October 31st,

NEW JUNCTION,

NEW SIGNAL BOXES AND NEW DOWN AND UP LOOP LINE PLATFORMS.

The New Down Facing and Up Trailing Junction put in about 150 yards North of Purley Station, forms a connection between the Down and Up Main Lines and the New Up and Down Junction Loop Lines at the North end of the Station, also with the Caterham and Chipstead Valley Branch Lines.

The Down Loop Line also connects with the Down Main Line at the South end of the Station. The Points and Signals leading from and to the Up and Down Main Lines will be worked from the two New Signal Cabins, viz., one at each end of the Station.

The Signal Box from which the Facing and Trailing Points leading to and from the Loop Lines at the North end of the Station will be worked, will be called the "North Cabin," and the Signal Box from which the Caterham Branch Facing and Trailing Points, on the Up and Down Loop Lines, together with the Trailing Points leading from the Down and Up Loop Lines, will be worked, will be called the "South Cabin."

The Ground Frame at the North end of the Station, from which the Points leading from the Down Siding to Down Main Line and the Points of the Main Crossover Road are worked, will be abolished.

The Single Line to and from Caterham and the Single Line to and from Chipstead will terminate near the South Eastern Company's New Signal Box at Purley, but the Single Line working will be controlled at that point, but the traffic will be worked in and out of Purley Station (L. B. & S. C. R.) by means of double lines.

The Old Signals which have been worked from the Brighton Company's Signal Box will consequently be removed, and the New Signals applicable to the Caterham and Chipstead Branch Lines will be worked from a New Signal Box, called Purley East, erected in the Fork between the Chipstead and Caterham Branch Lines by the South Eastern Company, and particulars of Points and Signals working therefrom will be given in due course by that Company.

Establishment of the freight yards south of Norwood Junction had been started in the late 1870s, becoming in time the main marshalling point for Brighton and then SR Central Section freight traffic. The Down yard was about a mile long, the sidings being in banks of seven or eight one beyond the other. The Up yard was similarly arranged though more limited in length by the tight curve of the Selhurst-Norwood Fork spur line into which it fitted. The yards were ideally placed to receive from and dispatch to all points of the compass and regularly hosted inter-company traffic from north of the Thames. These generally came via the West London line or the ex-LCDR's Metropolitan Extension, rather less often through the Thames tunnel.

The yards probably reached their zenith in the late 1930s. Despite best efforts by the Luftwaffe, and although some damage was caused, they were never put out of action during the hostilities though much housing round about as well as some nearby industrial sites suffered as I can personally testify. Much loss of life and personal injury resulted from these actions.

Wagonload traffic began really to fall away from the 1950s, and especially following the very damaging strike of 1955, though the yards survived in truncated form into the 1980s. The Down

yard has now all but vanished under natural re-colonisation, but much of the Up yard was absorbed over time by the extended Selhurst Traincare depot. The first part of this now very large installation had been erected in 1912 when the wires were extended here from Crystal Palace for servicing and berthing the new stock. Some of the original buildings are still in use, backing on to Selhurst Road and facing the entrance to Selhurst station.

Southern engines working in the yards were based mainly at New Cross Gate and West Croydon until Norwood Junction shed opened in 1935, permitting closure of West Croydon and transfer of some duties and engines from New Cross Gate. Herbert Walker had an intense dislike of the 'waste' of light engine working; the depot cost £33,125 but brought estimated savings of £2,000 pa from that source alone. Situated to the north of the station within the comforting embrace of the Down loop from Bromley Junction to the Brighton main line, its allocation was always of freight locos, principally of Brighton origin and usually between forty and fifty in number. It also took in the three Ashford-built 0-6-0DE shunters Nos 1-3 introduced in 1937, which remained there until (1520)2 was reallocated to Hither Green in the late 1950s.

Immediately before Nationalisation there were forty-six engines allocated to the shed, one of them oddly enough being motor-fitted 'D1' 0-4-2T No 2299. Whether this actually saw any service here seems doubtful. Otherwise, other than the diesels, there were only six engines not of Brighton origin. Twenty-four 'radial' tanks were predominant, five of them of Robert Billinton's first freight class, the 'E3'. No fewer than nineteen 'E4s' were on the books, including four rebuilt by Earle Marsh as 'E4x'. No 2473 was among this group, the former *Birch Grove*, now preserved at the Bluebell Railway and the sole survivor of Billinton's output. The ubiquitous 0-6-0 was represented by six of the strong 'C2x' and two insipid class 'C3' engines: two 'K' class moguls completed the Brighton lot. A single 'N' 2-6-0 and five of the massive 'W' class 2-6-4T conclude the then allocation.

In time, as the 'E3s' in particular were withdrawn, several 'Q' class 0-6-0s could be found there including No 549, the first to be fitted in BR days with a 'Standard class 4' blastpipe though then allied to a particularly austere stovepipe chimney. Several other members of the class received this modification in place of Bulleid's multi-jet system but those also had a Class 4 chimney which No 549 received later. After a short period when Maunsell moguls displaced by Kent Coast electrification found themselves in the unassuming environs of 75C, the shed closed in January 1964; its site was later cleared and occupied by Colas though presently it appears to be lying fallow.

Electrification has been touched on previously but to summarise; the overhead went live from Crystal Palace and through Norwood Junction to the works at Selhurst on 1 June 1912. A/C services out to Coulsdon North and Sutton via Thornton Heath began on 1 April 1925 following installation delays due to the war, though much of the work had been accomplished before the August 1914 outbreak. (The Sutton service had originally been planned to terminate at Cheam, which is why that station was built with 'through' lines

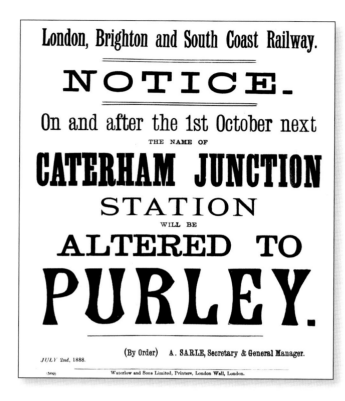

London, Brighton and South Coast Railway.

NOTICE.

On and after the 1st October next

THE NAME OF

CATERHAM JUNCTION

STATION

WILL BE

ALTERED TO

PURLEY.

JULY 2nd, 1888.

(By Order)   A. SARLE, Secretary & General Manager.

(500)   Waterlow and Sons Limited, Printers, London Wall, London.

between platform loops, but never got this far.) The overhead had been abandoned in its entirety in 1929, the last o/h train leaving Victoria for Coulsdon North at 10 minutes after midnight on Sunday 22 September that year. Third-rail services had been working alongside it since 17 June 1928, that installation also including the route between London Bridge and Epsom Downs via Streatham and Thornton Heath. Electrification at the same time of the spurs between Selhurst and Norwood Fork Junction permitted London Bridge to London Bridge 'circulars' via Peckham Rye, Streatham, Thornton Heath and Forest Hill.

Croydon's first third-rail services were actually to Addiscombe, a small part of the changeover on 28 February 1926 that took in much of the suburban area of the Eastern Section out of Charing Cross and Cannon Street. The Caterham and Tattenham Corner branches followed at electrification of the main London-Croydon line from 25 March 1928, trains from then on regularly working through to Tattenham Corner. History rears its head here because, despite Grouping, these branches were still looked on as SECR appendages and therefore their trains were worked to/ from the former SER's main London termini, Charing Cross and Cannon Street. But from June 1928 the peak-hour services were instead terminated at London Bridge. Herbert Walker wrote personally to every season ticket holder who used them explaining why this had become necessary, citing the build-up of traffic with increased electrification and the difficulty of pathing to/ from London Bridge's 'through' platforms. As might be expected, despite this courtesy, there were many vociferous complaints voiced and written. Off-peak 'through' working continued for many years more.

As noted already the West Croydon-Wimbledon line was energised on 6 July 1930. Waddon Marsh Halt opened that day too, a passing loop installed there breaking up the 4-mile long single line section between West Croydon and Mitcham Junction. The parallel freight line was never electrified. (Single passenger line token differentiation here for signalman and driver was straightforward, from West Croydon, a neat little baton: onward to Mitcham Junction, a massive shillelagh!)

Reopening of the Woodside-Selsdon line with third- rail power occurred on 30 September 1935 though the third rail went through to the next station, Sanderstead. The residents of that relatively affluent and influential suburb had long been complaining about the inadequacies of service on the Oxted line and the Southern, it may be assumed, considered this extension would answer those complaints. (Unlikely that it did!) However, the extension was not just to improve Sanderstead's services but also provide for the planned electric working of the incipient Surrey Heights Light Railway thence to Orpington. The poor financial situation at the beginning of the 1930s saw the project on hold and with the momentum lost and post-war Green Belt Acts controlling housing development this very possibly useful line died.

The first main line electrification was from Purley to Three Bridges and Reigate from 17 July 1932, Three Bridges-Brighton, Hove and Worthing following on 1 January 1933. We would have to wait five decades for the final phase of local electrification; the long-delayed installation from Sanderstead to East Grinstead opened for traffic on 5 October 1987, though sporadic electric services had worked since the line was fully energised in late-July. (The short section between South Croydon and Selsdon had gone 'live' in March 1984, permitting continuing termination of some trains at Sanderstead but reached off the main line.)

The thirty-eight signal boxes in use within the Borough at Grouping had been reduced to thirty at Nationalisation. Real change began in 1950 with colour-light signalling installed between Bricklayers Arms and Norwood North Junction, followed in October 1952 by conversion between Streatham Common and Selhurst which saw Thornton Heath box open only when access was required to the goods yard.

A particularly complex transfer came next, covering 'The Croydon Tangle' where lines from four directions meet. Two new power boxes, at Gloucester Road Junction and Norwood Junction, took over the work of six manual ones on 21 March 1954, though the limit was only to the south of Windmill Bridge Junction towards East Croydon, and St James's Junction on the L&CR route to West Croydon. These two boxes also controlled the connections to the marshalling yards and Selhurst depot.

Onward to Coulsdon North and the already track-circuit-equipped signalling to Brighton went live in May 1955. Power boxes for this installation were at East Croydon, South Croydon Junction and Purley. For the moment the manual Coulsdon North box was retained for shunting movements through the carriage sidings although the station's decline had already begun: for by this time it had long catered only for terminating local services. Weekend trains were withdrawn in 1965 and from

Purley North Down home and splitting distant signals. Note the Cologney Welch lamp to the left of the Down main distant.

What was then Corbett's Lane (more recently Rotherhithe New Road), near to the junctions of the London and Greenwich and London and Croydon railways.

1970 it came into use only in weekday peak-hours. The station closed officially on 3 October 1983 even if the last train had already left three days earlier. Smitham station, now Coulsdon Town after consultation with the local population as already noted, took over as a terminus during this period and continues to do so now, requiring a new trailing crossover to be installed.

Track circuit signalling was commissioned between West Croydon and Sutton in November 1972, Waddon box being among those closed; though both West Croydon boxes were retained *pro tem.* But the most significant change of recent years occurred with the 'Brighton Line Re-Signalling Scheme'. Under this, control of almost all the Croydon area was vested in a new signalling centre at Three Bridges. The London Bridge centre, fully commissioned by 1976, signalled the original London & Croydon line as far south as Norwood Junction while the Victoria Centre at Clapham Junction had control to Norbury.

The re-signalling was undertaken allied to major re-arrangement of track in the Croydon Tangle, which clearly showed their piecemeal development. For example, the original route through New Croydon to the Quarry Line was carrying the bulk of coastal traffic but at the same time was classified as 'Local' as that had been its original purpose pre-extension to Earlswood.

The re-arrangement was not only aimed at eliminating the 'local' double flat junctions beneath the main lines at Gloucester Road and that on the main line at the approach to Windmill Bridge Junction; even so, properly segregating 'local'

and 'main' traffic meant doing rather more than simply transposing the nomenclature of the two sets of track. Part of the problem also lay in the different 'pairing' of the four tracks north of Windmill Bridge, to London Bridge by direction, to Victoria by use. The loss of freight traffic between Selhurst and Norwood Junction meant the corresponding but lightly-used London Bridge-London Bridge circular passenger service over that route could be withdrawn and the relevant track removed. However, the connections that lead into/out of the Selhurst depot from these were naturally retained. Similarly, taking out the emergency spur between the main line at Selhurst and the West Croydon line at St James's Junction – the original main connection between the two routes pre-quadrupling – eliminated another very rarely-used piece of double track.

A new embankment went in north/ south across the whole site to carry Victoria line local trains for East Croydon to the east side of the layout at Windmill Bridge Junction. (Much of its substance was mining waste from Betteshanger colliery, and in that uncertain industrial time one of the several rumours circulating locally said this was coal being stockpiled in the event of a miners' strike.) In the embankment's course the London Bridge 'Fast' lines were crossed on a flyover, a link to the Up side of those lines named Cottage Junction put in immediately to the west. At the same time the triple junction at the head of the flyover at Norwood Fork was eliminated, leaving just a 'Down slow' to West Croydon – a direct return to atmospheric days! –

Passenger train East Croydon, c1905.

while the original Down Relief became the Down Slow to East Croydon. The works were completed in May 1984. The diagrams make clear how the track layout and classifications changed.

Sanderstead box closed when the Three Bridges Centre took over the signalling on the Oxted Line between South Croydon and Woldingham in 1985, leaving Addiscombe box – still semaphore equipped – as the last in the Borough. Unfortunately it was destroyed by fire in 1996, the branch from Elmers End then being worked as a 'one engine in steam' single line until its closure at the end of May 1997. A new Three Bridges Centre opened at Crawley in October 2013, still controlling the whole of the former SR Central Section south of Norwood Junction and Norbury.

Modern day rail services through the Town (August 2019) are dense and may possibly become more so if demand goes on growing and the Thameslink system continues to expand. Govia is the major but not the only franchisee. To take West

Croydon first by precedence: this station sees twelve northbound departures each off-peak hour: all but two are 'stoppers' on their respective routes. Six are destined for Victoria, four calling within the Borough at Selhurst, Thornton Heath and Norbury *en route via* Tulse Hill and Peckham Rye. The other two call at Norwood Junction which is also served by two 'fasts' going to London Bridge. The remaining four are worked by TfL Overground, the trains starting their journeys here for Highbury & Islington and also making their sole call within the Borough at Norwood Junction. In the Down direction four terminate at Sutton and two each at Epsom and Epsom Downs, all calling at Waddon before reaching the Sutton border. Two other Southern trains finish Down journeys here as do the four Overground services, all a very considerable advance on the timetable even as recently as twenty years ago.

Despite that intensity East Croydon is a very different

A panoramic view of Redhill at the point of divergence of the Brighton main line and Guildford routes.

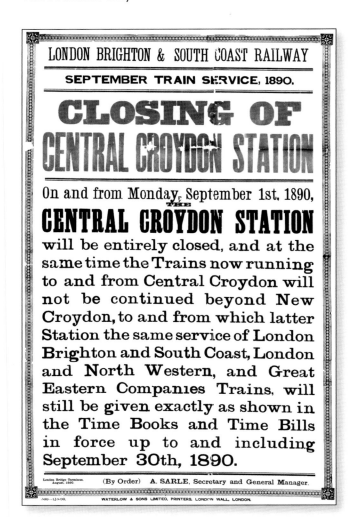

proposition, the third busiest station in London outside Zone 1. Northbound, each off-peak hour sees twelve trains go to Victoria, none of which call intermediately other than at Clapham Junction. Of the five that terminate at London Bridge, two slow trains serve Selhurst, Thornton Heath and Norbury within the Borough's boundary – as with those from West Croydon, travelling *via* Tulse Hill – two call only at Norwood Junction and one runs non-stop. The earlier-noted East Croydon/ Milton Keynes Central via Kensington and Watford Junction runs hourly, also calling at all three stations on the route to Clapham Junction. Thameslink now runs eight trains north per hour via Blackfriars; two of the four that go to Bedford now deign to call at Norwood Junction. But the two to Cambridge and two to Peterborough run direct to London Bridge.

As to Down workings, there is now no regular 'Brighton in the hour, on the hour' non-stop service, nor has there been for some years any pretence of one. Even the later 52-minute timing including calls at Clapham Junction and East Croydon has been phased out. Instead the six 'fast' trains per hour over the 40¼ miles south of the town take around 50 minutes and all call at Gatwick Airport which enjoys a level of service that must make the operators at Heathrow green with envy. Down trains that do call within the Borough hourly are the two to

East Grinstead that serve Sanderstead and Riddlesdown, and the two for Caterham and Tattenham Corner that spilt/join at Purley as was common for many years. These also take in South Croydon and Purley Oaks, the Tattenham Corner portion then calling at Reedham, Coulsdon Town and Woodmansterne while only Kenley on the Caterham branch is within the boundary. Caterham also sees another two trains hourly that call only at Purley and Kenley before crossing into Tandridge. Coulsdon has a regular service among its three stations, Coulsdon South seeing the twice hourly services to Horsham and Reigate, the latter also calling at Purley. A twice hourly train making calls at South Croydon, Purley Oaks and Purley terminates at Coulsdon South and Coulsdon Town alternately. Purley and Coulsdon South are also visited twice hourly by a 'slow' Gatwick service via Redhill.

Four longer distance 'conglomerates' run south but do not call anywhere else within the Borough. These are – hourly – Portsmouth Harbour and Bognor Regis; Littlehampton and Eastbourne; Southampton and Bognor Regis; and Ore and Littlehampton. The first and third of these are separated at Horsham, the other two at Haywards Heath. There is also the hourly Uckfield train that sprints up the hill to its first call, at Oxted, in thirteen minutes. In addition to all these, six 'Gatwick

Express' trains pass through each way hourly of which two southbound go on to Brighton.

The level of the present service raises a question on the earlier noted view that the Brighton Line is at about saturation point, especially at peak times. Punctuality figures tell only part of the story but suggestions on easing the situation are well up on the agenda though it must be emphasised these are as yet no more than that. They include two new platforms at East Croydon, possibly an island in the space once occupied by the sidings between the East and New stations. Additional track and further quite complex alterations to the junctions at Gloucester Road would be integral with this. Longer platforms similarly are on the cards though that would imply the need for similarly lengthened platforms where the main line trains call.

It is also suggested that, from a longer-term point of view, the Selsdon line be re-opened and upgraded with a new 'Gateway' station in the vicinity of South Croydon. Besides occupancy by Tramlink of the 4¼ miles between Coombe Road and Elmers End, the need for reinstatement of demolished infrastructure in the heart of Addiscombe, and quite intensive use by Hayes line trains beyond Elmers End, particularly in the peaks, all mean that route is hardly conducive to speedy travel.

The proposal apparently considered was that the route would continue from Lewisham northwards to tunnel beneath the Thames towards Canary Wharf and Stratford and thereby the ex-GER routes out of Liverpool Street, providing another North/South Crossrail corridor. Given this would still involve passage through the heavily-built up areas of the East and South-East London suburbs, the cost in terms of construction and compensation may prove unjustifiable.

Further out but aimed to relieve some of the pressure on the double track south of Balcombe, the reopening of the Uckfield-Lewes line, closed in 1969, was again examined in 2013 following an in-depth and non-committal report made in 2008. The Lewes by-pass now obstructs that line's approach to Lewes – the reason for its closure – but connection could still be achieved perhaps by reopening the original route, which passed north of the town to join the line from Keymer Junction, south of Cooksbridge. A north-to-west spur would have to be worked somewhere into the layout if it were intended trains travel directly to/from Brighton without reversal at Lewes. This could take the form of a tight 180° loop from east of the station, the track then running alongside the A27 to join the Brighton line south of the town. However, in view of the assessed price of such a spur and an apparent paucity of traffic that that might attract it would seem logical

H2 No 32421 *South Foreland* standing at East Croydon on 1 July 1950. *R C Riley/Transport Treasury*

Signals at South Croydon: all the distant signals having conventional lamps fitted.

to dispatch some Eastbourne and/ or Hastings services *via* Uckfield and the reopened section to the line from Keymer Junction because reversal would not be necessary for them. This locally-supported scheme would appear to have stalled because of its questionable cost/benefit rating. Moreover, with the best timings between Lewes and London via Uckfield – even with the line electrified – calculated at some 16-23 minutes more than from stations on the main line within easy driving distance, its attraction as a 'through' route would be limited. (If this were to come about, the re-opening of the Selsdon line might be more likely because of its direct access from/to the Oxted line.)

Quite how the problem of the heavy occupancy of the Brighton Line, one of the busiest in the country, and particularly on its way through the 'Tangle' bottleneck in the South London suburbs, may be solved is still at an early stage. The general and more strongly-expressed view appears to be investment in it rather than around it would produce the better result. Whatever the decided resolution, the problem will have to be addressed within the next two decades if traffic growth continues at present levels and the system is not to be overloaded well beyond its designed capacity.

Bibliography

History of the Southern Railway, C F Dendy Marshall, rev: R W Kidner, Ian Allan Ltd., 1963.

The London, Brighton & South Coast Railway, C Hamilton Ellis, Ian Allan Ltd., 1960.

The South Eastern & Chatham Railway, O S Nock, Ian Allan Ltd., 1961.

Sir Herbert Walker's Southern Railway, C F Klapper, Ian Allan Ltd., 1973.

Croydon's Railways, M W G Skinner, Kingfisher Railway Productions, 1985.

Railways of the Southern Region, Geoffrey Body, Patrick Stephens Ltd., 1984 (1989 edition).

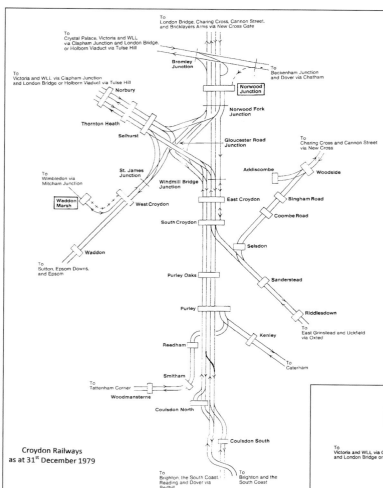

Croydon Railways
as at 31st December 1979

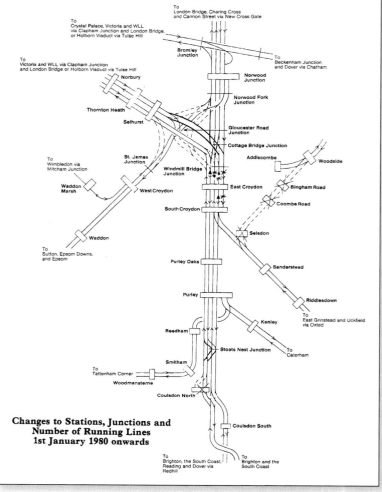

Changes to Stations, Junctions and
Number of Running Lines
1st January 1980 onwards

Southern Electric 1909-1979, G T Moody,
Ian Allan Ltd., 1957 (Revised 5th edition,
1979).

London Bridge to East Croydon, Vic Mitchell
and Keith Smith, Middleton Press, 1988.

Victoria to East Croydon, Vic Mitchell and
Keith Smith, Middleton Press, 1987.

London Bridge to Addiscombe, Vic Mitchell and
Keith Smith, Middleton Press, 1993.

Wimbledon to Beckenham – Before Tramlink,
John C Gillham, Middleton Press, 2001.

Caterham and Tattenham Corner, Vic Mitchell
and Keith Smith, Middleton Press, 1994.

Croydon (Woodside) to East Grinstead,
Vic Mitchell and Keith Smith, Middleton
Press, 1995.

Retracing the First Public Railway, Derek A
Bayliss, Living History Publications, 1981.

The Croydon, Oxted & East Grinstead Railway,
David Gould, The Oakwood Press, 2003.

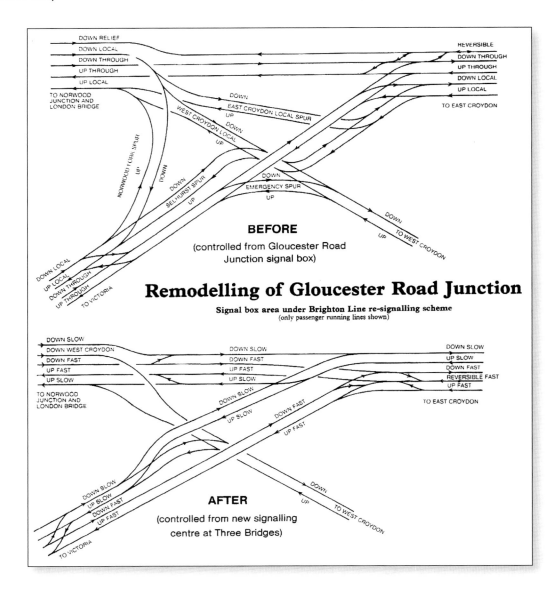

Remodelling of Gloucester Road Junction

Signal box area under Brighton Line re-signalling scheme
(only passenger running lines shown)

BEFORE
(controlled from Gloucester Road
Junction signal box)

AFTER
(controlled from new signalling
centre at Three Bridges)

'Rail', Bauer Media, April 2017.

Atlas of The Southern Railway, Richard Harman & Gerry Nichols, Ian Allan Publishing Ltd., 2016.

An Historical Survey of Southern Sheds, Chris Hawkins and George Reeve, Oxford Publishing Co., 1979.

ABC of Southern Locomotives, 11th ed., Ian Allan Ltd., 1947.

LBSCR Table of Distances, January 1901, Ian Allan Ltd., (undated reprint).

Pre-Grouping Railway Junction Diagrams, 1914, Ian Allan Ltd., (undated).

Railway Track Diagrams No 5, Southern & TfL, Edited by Gerald Jacobs, TRACKmaps, 2008 (3rd edition).

Ordnance Survey 1:50000 maps nos. 176, 177 and 187.

Croydon A-Z Street Atlas, Geographers' A-Z Map Co. Ltd., 2002.

I have consulted a number of websites, principally those to do with Croydon and its environs. But current Southern, Overground and Thameslink timetables have been scanned and personal visits made to stare at departure boards for an hour or so and take notes. A degree of confirmatory information has been provided by some other sites.

Rebuilt
The Letters and Comments Pages

New Identities? (SW48) Roger Merry-Price and Nigel Tilly have kindly both responded to my question from the Editorial of the above.

They refer to the case of the two M7s, Nos 30031 and 30128. No 30031 was withdrawn as No 30128 and cut up at Eastleigh whilst the original No 30128, complete with motor gear, and now renumbered No 30031, returned to traffic.

In addition in March 1961 No 30667 returned to traffic but had been originally No 30106. The real No 30667 was withdrawn in November 1960 and scrapped as No 30106. In both cases reference is the Peter Swift 'Book of the M7s' from Irwell Press.

Compiling 'Rebuilt' is one of the particular pleasures for your Editor. From the comments received I can sometimes judge the popularity (or otherwise) of various past inclusions as well as gaining much useful information for future content. It also allows for the inclusion of odd images, too good to ignore but which otherwise we might struggle to find a home for. An example is seen here; 'Marylebone – Brighton – Portsmouth – Waterloo', certainly a rail tour and one which we assume had the participants traversing various lines around London – or did they go further north before turning south? Any ideas would be welcome. (Regretfully no date.)

Nigel also takes things one stage further by referring to observation of components as well as using the example of the outside cylinders currently carried by 34039 which are stamped 34042. But Nigel then goes on to ask, "...does this mean the outer cylinders were removed and subsequently swapped at the same time?"

Chislehurst Goods Yard and SW Special 13. Our long term SW friend and contributor Jeremy Clarke has spotted an error within the above albeit going back a little while. "On page 7 there is a picture of Chislehurst goods yard (almost on my front step) with the final comment that it is now the station car park. Not so. It lies the best part of a quarter-mile north of the station, on the other side of a secondary main road (B264) and the site has been allowed to go wild for at least the last twenty-five years. (Check the satellite view on Google maps.) Car parking is along Station Approach on the Down side and on the recently reopened and resurfaced road up to what was once a dock behind the Up main platform."

We had a view of the carriage part of the 'Bug' earlier so here is the complete assembly. Not sure we can give too much credence to the headcode either whilst the location is also a little bit of a puzzler. No 58s (as she was then known) spent much time either stood at Eastleigh or taking the odd party around the Docks but is it Eastleigh on this occasion?

SW48 and some more locations as well as No 563, again from Jeremy Clarke.

"There is no doubt the picture of No 383 on page 90 was taken at Clapham Junction. Note the oil-lit Stroudley 'perishable goods' vans in the Exchange Siding on the right.

I tend not to go through 'SW' front to back but pick up here and there so I've just come upon Mr Townroe's Archives. I recollect dear old Uncle Mac telling me that No 563 went up to Waterloo hauling the restored Tri-composite with a maximum of 60psi in the boiler. Speed was restricted, I think to 25mph, though that's uncertain.

What else? Well, the caption to the photo of the atmospheric pipes on P22; one of the three pumping stations was on the Down side north of Norwood Junction. It was demolished to make way for the long-closed spur line arriving from Birkbeck, opened on 18 June 1862. Local rumour had it that one of the small factories that backed on to the main line here contained much of the stonework from it. The Croydon Waterworks building raised from material from the Croydon pumphouse is still in place behind Surrey Street. It is Grade II listed, presently privately-owned though not currently in use."

And don't forget to read the last contribution in this section from Alan Kinge who also picks up on the story of No 563 – Ed.

Some reminisces from Ernie Oliver. We always enjoy hearing memories such as these so do please keep them coming... .

"Hello Kevin, I am a relative newcomer to SW, finding my first copy in a well-known chain of bookshops. I was immediately 'smitten' and have slowly been catching up with

Courtesy of Roger Merry-Price we have this image of D1 No 256 working on the Western Section at Seaton Junction and seen here with the branch train of gate stock.

all the back numbers and specials as time (and money) permit.

I am currently reading issue 40, so I still have a little catching up to do. Although I am now in my mid-70s, I can't pretend to be anywhere near as knowledgeable as the vast majority of your correspondents, but here goes anyway. I have always lived in the Southern Region area. Originally in Welling on that little backwater known as the Bexleyheath line, which ran past the back of my parents' house a quarter of a mile or so on the up side of Welling Station. I now live in Waterlooville, Hampshire (no trains at the back of my house now unfortunately). However, I have always had a sneaking preference for the Eastern section of the Southern Region. Roughly the area covered by the old SE&CR.

In amongst the 4-SUB, 2- & 4-EPB sets, (and of course the two unique 4DD, which I always think sounded rather 'tinny') that made up the bulk of the unglamorous Bexleyheath Line traffic, occasionally we did get the odd little bit of excitement: I fondly remember 'C' Class 0-6-0s on pick-up freights, and the occasional ex-LBSC 'C2X' Class 0-6-0 on similar duties and even the very occasional 'W' Class 2-6-4T. On one memorable occasion the appearance of an 'O1 Class' 0-6-0 (I distinctly remember the outside framed tender). Unfortunately I did not take any numbers, and the cost of buying a film for the family 'box brownie' was far beyond my 2/6d a week pocket money. Other things that stayed with me were on summer Saturdays/Sundays seeing ancient ex-SECR 4-4-0s struggling up the 1 in 198 out of Welling station with return summer excursions from the Kent coast and a string of equally ancient pre-Grouping coaches, mostly in green but the occasional one in red livery. One summer's day, my parents took us on a day trip to Margate. We were in the front coach, which was a 'birdcage' brake with a side corridor. My father and I ventured into the unlocked Guard's compartment, where we climbed up into the birdcage and peered out over the top of the tender, getting cheery waves from the driver and fireman.

I also remember very soon after Winston Churchill's funeral in 1965 seeing (his?) brown and cream bogie utility van parked in the sidings at Blackheath with the dreaded circular 'Condemned' symbol on the side. Or did they paint any other utility vans in those colours?

The other thing I remember back in the 50s was getting a direct train to Brighton on Summer Saturdays or maybe Sundays. This train was usually formed of 2-BIL and/or 2-HAL units, reversed at London Bridge, and then proceeded down the main line to Brighton. I do not know how long it ran for, but I occasionally saw it pass the back of our house

Talking of Kent coast excursions. A memory that will always stay with me (though I am not a diesel fan) was

that fateful day of Sunday 11 June 1972, when Class 47 No 1630 came to grief on the tight curve at Eltham Well Hall with a return excursion from the Kent coast. We were all sitting in our lounge watching TV, when we were suddenly assailed by a distant 'growl' that grew louder and louder to a crescendo, shaking the house as it went past. (Most trains that passed the back of my parent's house were usually either picking up speed from, or slowing for, Welling Station.) "By Gum – He's going some!" my dad exclaimed – well we all know what tragically happened a couple of miles further on down the line! *(Detail on the tragedy referred to by Ernie may be found in the formal enquiry report accessible from the excellent 'Railways Archive' website at* https://www.railwaysarchive.co.uk/documents/ DoE_Eltham1972.pdf)

One last thing – as I do not want to run the risk of inflicting terminal boredom on you. The first steam-hauled railtour I participated on, back in 1963, was the 'Scottish Bluebell' from Victoria to the then fledgling Bluebell Railway, featuring T9 120, and, of course, Caledonian Railway single no 123. I never cease to be amazed that the opportunity was never taken to use this loco on other tours while visiting the Southern Region. How did it get down south? Did it come down Light Engine? Double-headed with another loco? I am pretty sure it didn't work down hauling a train on its own. Does anyone out there have the answer? (Nowadays it would probably come on a low-loader.)"

Southern 4 SUB compartment interior. Oh the sensation of hip-bones being pressed together…of bags slipping off the knees…of looking down before attempting to move the feet … and then treading on (or being trod upon) as someone entered or vacated. Do we miss it – not really!

We have responded to Ernie's question about the Caledonian single as best we can; as probably light engine. But can anyone provide a more definite statement please?

Now a few locomotive points raised by Eric Youldon re SW48. Eric also confirms the S15s were fitted for steam heat. Eric also suggests the caption on page 2 referring to the rear cover view is in fact that for a Waterloo – Bournemouth train. Sorry Eric, I would still disagree; in the example shown the disc is not at the top of the smokebox but centre right instead. Next is the view of T9 No 336 with what we now know is the tender from a '700', so a definite LSWR combination. Finally we are correct on page 95 with the date the L12s went to the Eastern Section. This was 1925 and not, as erroneously stated, 1930.

Now a few valid points from Nick Stanbury re SW48. "Page 5: I do not know the location but that shunt signal appears to be of typical LBSCR (not LSWR) revolving pattern, with the 'L' possibly indicating 'Loop' or 'Local'. But the 'notice' poses more questions than answers and its true application is unclear, at least to me. Is it a warning to staff on foot that 'walking' clearances under the bridge are tight, in which case why do 'high box trucks' require special mention? Or is it a prohibition on the passage of anything on rail other than 'low' vehicles because of restricted headroom? In either case, the wording ought to read '… ENGINES, TRAINS …' to be grammatical and consistent, if still uncertain in its message.

Then to page 45: there seems to be little doubt that the S15s were fitted for steam heating as they were frequently used on passenger trains, and not just in the summer months. There is photographic evidence (including that at pp44-5) of them with steam-heating pipes.

And finally to Page 82: it is likely that the train shown is the RCTS 'Holborn Viaduct to Victoria' rail tour on 30 September 1950, for which No 31102 was the motive power for at least the initial short run to Cannon Street (as per the 'Six Bells' website). The guard (third from left) appears to be Bill Crawforth, still wearing his Southern Railway uniform. He often worked such specials on South London and Central Division lines and was an organiser of those run by the Southern Counties Touring Society." (*Sorry we missed that one on 'Six Bells' so for anyone wanting the full details please refer to* https://www.sixbellsjunction.co.uk/ *– Ed.*)

Now from Alan Kinge re No 563 and John Francis, page 61 SW48. We mentioned in the associated caption to No 563 on page 61 the name John Francis. It transpired this was a man who would have had a story to tell. Sadly he is no longer with us but very fortunately Alan Kinge regularly met John and was able to recall some of their conversations.

This view has recently arrived from Ian Nolan concerning Graham Hatton's Permanent Way notes from pages 93/94 in SW8 and page 103 of SW14. Ian comments the view is of Paddock Wood and shows the Up main line receiving the same treatment as in the article. The question being, is this a military man wearing the cap on the footplate, or a railway issue cap of the period? No details as to the locomotive involved.

Some more recently received images, this time from David Lindsell under the heading 'Steam Commuting in the 1960s'. "Back in the sixties the number of commuters from Andover to London Waterloo was a lot less than they are today. Commuting probably started somewhere around Woking and has gradually spread to places as far away as Salisbury and Southampton. The pictures show bowler hatted commuters about to board the 07.49 Salisbury to Waterloo service fronted by rebuilt Pacific No 34052 *Lord Dowding* on a cold Tuesday 26 April 1966. No 34052 was built at Brighton Works in January 1946 and rebuilt at Eastleigh in September 1958. It was a Salisbury engine from 1951 until withdrawn in July 1967 and scrapped at Cashmores in South Wales in February 1968. In the yard we can see Standard Class 4 No 80082 paused between shunting duties. She also hailed from Brighton, this time in 1954 and lasted in service until September 1966. Scrapping took place in January 1967 also at Cashmores.

These two pictures were taken by local Andover lad Eddie Field, who attended college in Basingstoke at this time and they now form part of my photographic collection. Note that there is also a train in the down platform which, according to Eddie's notes, was probably worked by 34019 *Bideford* an un-rebuilt Bullied Pacific."

"I first met John in 1971 whilst working for Anthea Williams – Corinthian Coaches. He was a regular passenger on the Hiltingbury (Chandlers Ford) Women's Institute trips – which also attracted just as many husbands! I think this was due to the scheduled 'coffee stops', etc, which were usually 'public house' stops...need I say more?

John was by then 93 years old. He had been born near Shepton Mallet in 1878 but later his father moved to St Denys, Southampton, where he attended the new St Denys school. Leaving school in 1892 he obtained a job on the railway and a little while later became a cleaner at Northam shed. He recalled having to clean the two engines involved in Queen Victoria's funeral train from Gosport to Fareham where they handed over to the LBSCR for the onward journey to London.

Later in April 1912 he was by then a young fireman working from Eastleigh and was on the footplate of a tank engine given the task of pulling the empty stock out of a berth opposite No 143. This was one of several special trains from Waterloo carrying passengers from London who sailed on the *Titanic*. He even recalled watching her sail...

As a fireman he also remembered working on Drummond's 'Bug', whilst also confirming the known belief that Drummond himself was 'quite loud and sharp'.

John seems also to have been involved in some unusual workings such as the making of the 1927 film 'The Ghost Train' between Longparish and Wherwell on the little used branch between Hurstbourne and Fullerton. The train was painted white. *(Several versions of this film have been made – Ed.)*

By 1929/30 he was a driver trusted for Royal Train duties and recalled the occasion when the Duke of York (later to become King George VI), the Duchess of York and the young Princess Elizabeth rode on the footplate of an engine from Waterloo to Clapham Junction. A photograph was taken of John holding the present Queen up so she could see out of the

front of the cab; some years later a copy of the photograph was given to John by BR.

Sometime around the mid-thirties he was in charge of the train that took the King of Afghanistan non-stop from Waterloo to Portland, at the time an almost unique run, there being only a few drivers with the route knowledge throughout.

During WW2 he was promoted and from what follows this was likely to the post of a Loco Running Inspector based at Eastleigh. He recalled one night meeting the driver of a freight train that had arrived at the east yard and enquiring of the driver if they had had a good run down. When the driver replied in the affirmative John suggested to the driver he return to Micheldever to collect the remainder of his train which had literally been blown into two sections when a German bomber dropped a few bombs on the line between the two tunnels; in all the noise the crew had failed to notice the end of their train was missing!

It is very likely that it was around the time of WW2 that he came into contact with SCT and although ordinarily he would have retired through age around 1943 he continued on until the end of WW2. Because of the contact between the two men during those times it was for this reason he was probably present at the steaming of No 563.

John was widowed prior to WW2 but he remarried having met the lady who was to be his second wife in 1946/7, this whilst on a cruise. When later asked, on his 100th birthday, for the best memory during his long life, he replied it was going in the lift to the top of the Empire State Building especially when it showed 'non-stop'. John also had a son who was a director of a company in Cambridge.

Alan Kinge attended John's 100th Birthday party in 1978 and he is pretty certain Stephen Townroe was also present – we used to carry him as well on the WI trips. Alan also noticed the two men often in conversation.

John lived to be 106 and was alert to the end."

No 563 in later times at Brighton. *Norman Simmons*

And finally from Peter Jordan, again on the subject of No 563. Peter wrote originally to refer us to some further detail available in 'MacLeod's Other Island' back now, and what it specifically says about the T3:

"Mac was also beavering away behind the scenes with the Waterloo Centenary event, and with a small team he selected LSWR T3 class loco No 563 from the scrap line at Kimbridge for display. They made the selection on site on 4 May and by the 28th of the month the loco was at Eastleigh with a tube change and base coat painting well under way. The event was to be opened by Herbert Walker on 14 June, so there was little time for delay, and whilst Helen McKie had many months to prepare her wonderful 'Waterloo Centenary' posters and cover for the illustrated booklet, the painters at Eastleigh must have been really at their wits end with the tri-composite coach and locomotive. A little tacky varnish could be forgiven!"

We regret we could not find an image of P C McCloud, but as he will forever be associated with the Isle of Wight railways why not an IOW view. This one is Ventnor in 1965.

The book also reproduces the specification that was drawn up for the restoration, which reads as follows:

"Turbett *(the Eastleigh Works Manager),* Townroe and painter foreman Miller and I went to Kimbridge Junction on 4 May and inspected the row of engines awaiting removal to Dinton for cutting up. There were four Adams 4-4-0 engines, all with 6' 7" driving wheels, Nos 563, 572 – T3s and 658 and 666 – X6 class, in the siding.

We all agreed that No 563 should be selected for preservation. The engine will be sent to Eastleigh and alterations made as follows:

Adams chimney to be fabricated and fitted

Two cast-iron number plates of Adams style to be made and affixed to cab sides

Two whistles to be added and pipework replaced

The engine need only be complete externally.

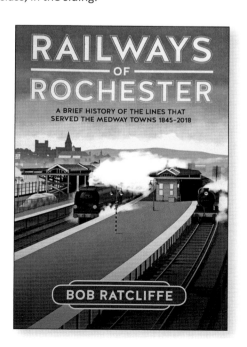

I have left the following with Mr Mills, Chief Draughtsman, who is co-ordinating the work:

Photograph of engine 661 – *Railway Magazine* coloured plate showing Drummond painting of LSW 395.

Two transfer Ellis coats of arms to be used on 563 and a photographic card of No 561 showing the condition in which the engine is to be preserved.

Left with Mr Allen photograph of tri-compo. coach No 633, a similar coach will be preserved and painted in salmon pink and plain chocolate.

A copy of painting details of LSW engine in Drummond style and coach were left with Mr Mills (locomotive) and Mr Hurleigh (carriage) side."

Although the above says that the locomotive need only be complete externally, the book makes it clear that the boiler had its tubes changed so, presumably, was deemed to be in sound condition. This suggests that, as the engine had been 'dry stored' for a long time the boiler may still have been reasonably sound.

A new book which readers may not be aware of is *Railways of Rochester* by the late Bob Ratcliffe. Copies are available either from the City of Rochester Society at £20.00 + £3.50pp, or direct from Andy Ratcliffe on andyratcliffe67@gmail.com

The Lines and Stations Dr Beeching Did Not Close:
Further Notes From Richard Simmons Reference SW42

May I add another section of line which has not been closed but over which passenger services were withdrawn but the line not closed, and did not make it into the list in SW42? I refer to the relatively short spur between Point Pleasant Junction (between Wandsworth Town and Putney) and East Putney, which the October 1960 Western Section Appendix to the Working Time Table lists as being 1,339 yards long.

I suppose this spur was unusual in that except for a short section in East Putney station, both Down and Up lines did not share the same formation. The Down line left the Down Windsor slow line at Point Pleasant Junction climbing sharply up to its own platform at East Putney where the Up line also had its own platform, both separate from adjoining LUL District Line platforms. After leaving the station the line crossed over all four Windsor lines before descending to and trailing into the Up Windsor line at Point Pleasant Junction.

I am sure readers will be aware that the spur formed part of the route of the L&SWR pioneering electrification scheme

between Waterloo and Wimbledon via East Putney inaugurated in 1915. Introduction of such schemes are usually associated with regular interval Sir Herbert Walker type 'clock face' timetables replacing rather haphazard and irregular steam hauled services. I suppose the only exception to this rule was the steam-operated regular interval service on the Oxted group of lines – not then decimated by Beeching – introduced in the summer 1956 timetable and subsequently taken over by 'Oxted' DEMUs (late Class 207) when they were constructed.

I have a copy of the 1939 Southern Railway summer timetable from which it is seen the concept of a regular interval frequency did not apply totally to Waterloo-Wimbledon via East Putney services, many of which turned back at Wimbledon Park where they no doubt laid over in depot sidings before returning to Waterloo; there was no Sunday service.

In line fashion we struggled to find an early image around the area now under discussion, so the first alternative is this of Battersea cabin a few miles distant.

To be followed by No 30577 running light and we think was taken at the time of the special train described in the text.

Passenger services did not, however, survive WW2 and *the London Railway Atlas 4th Edition* by Joe Brown, published by Ian Allan in 2000, showed it as being withdrawn in May 1941, and has never been restored. Even so, after withdrawal of regular passenger services the line did not in fact become moribund and continued to be used for empty stock movements from Waterloo after the morning peak; that is for trains not required again before the evening peak.

The last Carriage Working Notice I have is that for South West Trains produced covering the period 29 September 2003 to 21 November 2003 edition which shows, Saturdays excepted, nine Down trains from Waterloo to Wimbledon Park depot via East Putney and three in the opposite direction for the evening peak. There are also several Down trains in the late evening at close of service together with several Up trains in the early morning for start of service. All avoiding possible congestion if the entrance/exit on the main line at Earlsfield was otherwise used. Following withdrawal of loaded regular passenger services, as well as the aforementioned empty trains, the spur continued to be used from time to time for diversions during planned engineering work together with special trains and some van trains off the main line in need of reaching the Windsor line side of Clapham Junction, such as those conveying Hampshire fruit traffic to which I referred to in my article "Strawberries and Steam" in SW39.

There was also a reminder that milk was once conveyed by rail as in the May 1969 – May 1970 Working Time Table. In this I came across a 13.58 Wimbledon West Yard-Clapham Junction via East Putney empty milk tank train which started back from Morden South on Saturdays, by now of course diesel- hauled.

I travelled on one such special train on 23 November 1952 when the Railway Correspondence and Travel Society organised a special service, 12.38 Waterloo to Brookwood via East Putney hauled by venerable Adams '0395' 0-6-0 30577. Following arrival at Brookwood, participants changed into one of two special trains to Bisley Camp formed of M7 0-4-4T 30027 and pull and push 'gate' set No 363. For rolling stock expert readers the train from Waterloo was formed of 'Sheppey' sets Nos 513 and 514 and three-set 406. I don't know what significance set No 406 had, the formations being taken from the relevant printed Special Traffic notice.

Unfortunately the spur became restricted to Down trains only from 4 April 1987 because of the deteriorating structure of the Up line flyover spanning the four Windsor lines, this bridge being subsequently demolished. Nevertheless, as part of the Waterloo Area Resignalling Scheme of the time (WARS), the Down line was resignalled for reversible working due to have come into effect on 11 February 1991 but subsequently delayed until 24 February 1991 because of, according to my note on the relevant signalling yellow notice, 'Arctic weather conditions'.

As part of the same scheme, Point Pleasant 2 Junction and East Putney signal boxes were closed on 16 September 1990 and 24 February 1991 respectively, coming under control of Wimbledon ASC, although the former Wimbledon 'A' box controlled the East Putney line only between 15 April 1990 and 24 February 1991.

So when did passenger-carrying trains return? Not as a result of any resumption of the Waterloo-East Putney – Wimbledon service but instead in the form of a couple of 'Parliamentary' Waterloo-Basingstoke stoppers, ie those which are semi fast to Woking then all stations to Basingstoke, run half hourly but only one of the two per hour call at Clapham Junction.

It was quite by accident that when thumbing through timetables I noticed that the 23.12 Waterloo-Basingstoke was allowed an inordinate amount of time compared with others between Clapham Junction and Surbiton and I was unable to fathom out why but did wonder if it was routed via East Putney. It must have been given this generous amount of time for some years, because I recall attending one of the 2012 Olympia evening events and hoping to return to Farnborough on the 23.12, but it didn't happen. On another occasion I attended an evening performance at the Royal Albert Hall assuming that on this occasion the timing of the end would give me the opportunity of travelling on the 23.12, but disappointment for the second time.

The mystery was, however, resolved early last autumn. My son is an ardent fan of Arsenal football team, attending their home evening matches from time to time. He usually telephones me in the late evening to check up on his 'old Dad', and one evening duly phoned me to say he had attended one such evening match and was sitting at Waterloo on the 23.12 to return to Farnborough. I lost no time in requesting him to take note of the route followed to see if it passed through East Putney! I had to explain the reason for this as he could not understand why I wanted to know, and then to let me know when he telephoned the following evening. I did not have to wait that long because about half an hour later he sent me a text to say the train had just passed through Southfields!

Insofar as the opposite direction is concerned, from the timetable I could not recognise any timing between Surbiton and Clapham Junction which suggested a particular train was routed via East Putney.

But everything comes to he who waits and it must have been about two years ago that part of the 04.54 Basingstoke – Waterloo became partially derailed at slow speed when leaving Wimbledon after its scheduled stop. For a few mornings following the derailment local radio stations traffic reports warned that LUL District Line trains were not operating to Wimbledon because of track repairs following the derailment. So how did a derailment on the main line affect District Line trains to Wimbledon? The answer to this conundrum came many months later when the inspecting officer's official report attributed the derailment to defective track on the short stretch connecting the main line to the East Putney line. So the 04.54 ex-Basingstoke runs via East Putney and further timetable study does indicate additional time for the train between Wimbledon and Clapham Junction.

The final question is when did it become possible again for passengers to travel over the Point Pleasant Junction – East Putney spur? With only a public timetable available it can be difficult to give definitive answers because, for instance, I found that at some stage in its existence, the 04.54 ex-Basingstoke ran non-stop from Surbiton to Vauxhall, the only such train of the day, it seems, to do this whilst 'guestimates' have also to be made from time to time. But again, judging purely from the public timetables the 23.12 ex-Waterloo has run via East Putney since the 2011 summer timetable but the 04.54 ex-Basingstoke was before that. In fact I suspect it is certain that routing these two trains this way has been deliberately done to enable train crews to retain route knowledge for possible diversions, even though the East Putney line was transferred from BR to LUL ownership in April 1994.

Finally I think it worth recalling that this Waterloo-Wimbledon service was withdrawn over 70 years ago when in Southern Railway ownership when station and line closures were made at the whim of the owning railway company and not subject to the regulatory closure procedure that we became all too familiar with post-nationalisation.

Finally another London area image – the fogman at work. The gap in the conductor rails, so he might put down replacement detonators, is almost the only concession to Health & Safety.

Frant Station

Arthur Percival

For some years 'SW' has been supported not just by its subscribers but also by the casual buyer at various retail outlets. In the latter case this helps us all, including the retailer, whether that be the bookshop at your favourite heritage railway or on the High Street courtesy of the local independent outlet.

One of these independent outlets has for many years been the Faversham Society and their premises at the Fleur de Lis Heritage Centre in the town. (Blatant plug but why not!)

It has also not been just a one-way traffic as some little time back we were privileged to receive from them copies of some images contained in a family album. Other than that they relate to Frant station we know little else. Period is variable but we would guess from the late Victorian era through to the early years of the 20th century. Sadly no full details although it is possible the family name in some was 'Lavender'. As these are also literally no more than snapshots in the family album the quality is variable. Even so a fascinating record which it is a pleasure to share.

We are extremely grateful to Arthur Percival of the Faversham Society for bringing these to our attention.

Above left: **'Railway Officials' at Frant c1898(?), likely the Station Master and possibly a signalman.**

Above right: **The station is located on the Hastings line of the former SER between Grove Junction and Wadhurst. Built to the design of the SEC Architect William Tress, we can date this tinted view as post-1905; the time the canopy was added.**

The small signal box at the station. As was the practice for the SECR,, the platforms were staggered with the signal box on the down side of the line.

We are now looking towards Wadhurst with the Up siding on the right.

Right: **Possibly a member of the Lavender family.**

Below: **Ganger and platelayers to the north of the station in the area of the goods yard.**

Bottom: **Finally a Hastings line freight approaches the station. Passenger facilities on the Up side were distinctly spartan.**

Eastleigh 8 August 1966

Tony Harris

For some little time now, Tony Harris has been quietly sending us images from his spotting days 50+ years ago.

Here we are delighted to portray a selection from that visit; a time when engines were falling by the wayside in ever increasing numbers and the melancholy sight of withdrawn locomotives awaiting that final trip west to South Wales and oblivion was increasing almost on a daily basis.

Above: **We start our views with No 34017 *Ilfracombe* captured from Platform 3 with a Waterloo bound express. There was little to differentiate the Bournemouth/Weymouth line services, as all carried the same headcode (certainly as far as Bournemouth) whilst only two were given the honour of headboards – 'The Bournemouth Belle' and 'The Royal Wessex' – and even then these were not always carried. The well photographed notice advising loco men not to walk on the lines to the shed but instead to use the road is on the right. Conductor rails are either laid or awaiting attention whilst an MAS bracket, as yet without its signal heads, has been erected.**

Opposite top: **Powering through on the Up main is D6578 with vans. The thin sheet encasing the front end already shows signs of damage, a feature that was common to all members of the class.**

Bottom: **The USA tanks were not just based at Southampton Docks, as in their later years and coinciding with the shortage of more normal shunting engines, they could also be found on transfer freight workings between the various yards at Eastleigh. Here No 30069 waits in platform 3 probably having come from the East yard which despite its name was situated at the north end of the station. Eastleigh West signal box is in the background as well as a DEMU set standing in the up siding.**

D2998, again a type more usually found on Dock shunting but captured here resting between duties opposite platform 4. One of the two Eastleigh yard ground frames may be seen in the background.

To the depot now and which in its final year was host to Bulleid locos, Standards, Ivatt 2-6-2T types and the USA class, these representing all that was left of the erstwhile steam fleet. No 75077 looks as if it is being prepared for duty, the tender piled high and the cylinder cocks blowing through so it may in fact just be starting to move.

At the rear of the shed, No 41287 stood out of steam coupled to No 73170. Both had been withdrawn, No 73170 in June, and No 41287 in July. As yet the latter at least still retains its motion.

Another engine never to steam again, No 34097, formerly *Holsworthy* but already out of use for four months and seen awaiting its final rail movement. This would be to the South Wales scrapyard of Messrs Cashmore and where it was broken up just one month later.

The period was also witness to what seemed (to the regular visitor at least) an almost endless number of Mogul types, all withdrawn. At the rear of the shed is U No 31639, withdrawn in June 1966 after a working life of just over 35 years. It too met its end at Cashmores.

A side view of No 73170 seen earlier, which had a working life of just over nine years, hardly what had been intended and certainly not a cost-effective investment for British Railways.

Another Mogul, this time an example of the N class, the principal difference from the U being that of different size driving wheels, Most of the Moguls were very run down by the time they ceased work and whilst they could certainly have been repaired for further use, either their work had been taken over by diesels or the traffic they had once catered for had been lost from rail.

Finally to Eastleigh station again and a visitor in the form of LMS 'Black 5' No 44942 (perhaps that should really be 'grimy 5') at the head of a down inter-regional service at platform 3. The buildings behind were soon to be demolished to be replaced by a two storey 'clasp' building. This looked terrible in 1967 and is even worse 50+ years later.

Field Trip to Bembridge

Alan Postlethwaite

We are delighted to include another in this series from Alan which explores lines closed many years previous.

All uncredited photographs are by the author and are copyright of the Bluebell Railway Photographic Archive.

For railway photos of Brading, St Helens and Bembridge taken in the late 19th century and early 20th century, I can recommend Peter Paye's book, 'Isle of Wight Railways Remembered', published by Oxford Publishing Co. in 1984.

The train ferry, PS *Carrier*, arriving at Langstone Harbour after crossing from St Helens Quay. *Painting by the late Les Henson*

On St Helens seafront, this rake of Metropolitan Railway rigid six-wheelers found a new lease of life as beach huts. All aboard for Baker Street!

I walked the Bembridge branch on a chilly overcast day in April 1960. Starting at Brading, the first delight was St Helens station building. Looking remarkably grand for a single line, its fine architecture was somewhat spoiled by the great canopy and frontal drain pipe. St Helens quay was for freight so passenger traffic here would have been mainly local villagers and a trickle of summer visitors. This building became a residence.

Opening in 1878, the Brading Harbour Improvement and Railway Company built a railway line from Brading to St Helens where the Isle of Wight Marine Transit Company initiated a train-ferry paddle steamer service to Langstone Harbour on the Haying Island branch of the LB&SCR. Launched in 1858, the ferry, PS *Carrier*, had seen earlier service on the Firth of Tay before the bridge was built and again after its collapse. When the St Helens train ferry scheme failed financially, the ferry was sold and the railway line was taken over by the IWR in 1898.

St Helens station was just inland from the quay. This photo shows not the leaning tower of Pisa but a gas holder of the gas works. The line to St Helens quay went straight ahead, splitting into the North and South quays. The extension to Bembridge branched to the right. Imports at St Helens quay included coal and flour. Exports included cement from the mill which was located on Brading quay. When the railway embankment to Bembridge was built, this allowed land to be drained and reclaimed along the route and Brading ceased to be a port.

As well as St Helens freight traffic, the railway served the select tourist resort of Bembridge whose station building was substantial. Its great canopy covered the signal box as well as the platform. The turntable, located just beyond the platform, was enlarged in 1936 to accommodate the newly arrived L&SWR class O2 tanks. A siding to the right handled general goods. A siding to the left was used mainly for coal.

There was no canopy on the forecourt of Bembridge station, only a weighing machine. The entrance doorway is also surprisingly modest. The date in the brickwork is 1877, five years before the station opened. The branch closed in 1953 and this site was later redeveloped with housing.

Left: Brading signal box had a Stevens frame and windows but the tall outline may have been an IWR design. The valance is a delightful touch.

Below right: In 1960, open saloons with bench seats were an attractive feature of some island trains. This one is on a modified SE&CR coach.

Below left: This Stroudley goods brake van found a new lease of life as a beach hut at St Helens. Shall we brew some tea after a quick dip?

Bembridge trains terminated at the outer face of Brading's island platform. Adams class O2 tank No. 31 *Chale* restarts with a train to Ryde.

Five Specials Ascend 'The Alps' Part 2
'The Dorset Belle' Railtour
Les Price
(All images by the author unless stated otherwise)

No 35028 *Clan Line* **soon to depart from Waterloo. As yet the platform starting signal has yet to be cleared otherwise the word 'OFF' would appear in the indicator box.**

Having previously narrated details of the first two assaults on 'The Alps', by the 'S15' (page 84 et seq. SW49), we now come to the next, the LCGB 'Dorset Belle' railtour of 27 February 1966, also the third such train to run via 'The Alps' in the first quarter of 1966.

This was quite a memorable rail tour since it covered lines I had never traversed before and the ban on steam on what was then Western Region territory west of Salisbury had been specially lifted for our benefit. A round trip behind steam of almost 335 miles was certainly one to savour.

Eager participants arrived at Waterloo in good enough time to see Merchant Navy Class 'Pacific' No 35028 *Clan Line* back

down on to her nine coach rake. This comprised a BSK, 3 SOs, an RB, 3 more SOs and a BSK. *Clan Line* was well turned out and appeared 'in good nick'. There was an air of anticipation; how would she perform 'over the Alps'?. .And later what about Toller bank behind a pair of tank engines?

In its Introduction to the itinerary booklet for the tour, the LCGB set out its aims for the day: *"The 'Dorset Belle' not only covers considerable parts of the two main lines to Weymouth, but also penetrates two branch lines and uses a little-known wartime connection."*

We duly left Waterloo on time at 9am. We had been allocated a very gentle schedule for the first part of the journey; an hour and four minutes to cover the 46 miles 48 chains to Alton, our expected first stop, hence we proceeded very sedately down the LSWR main line to Pirbright Junction.

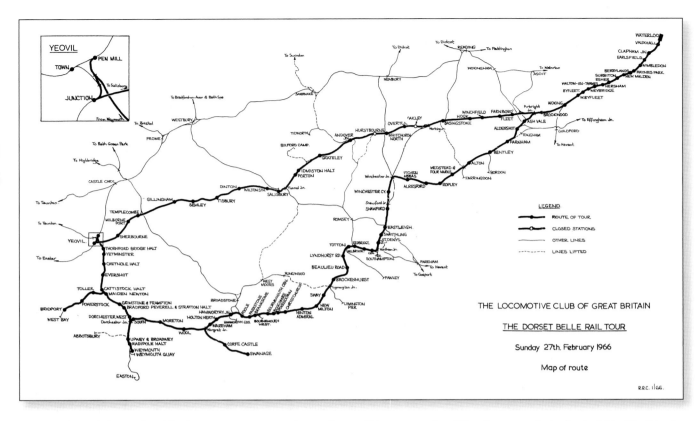

YEOVIL

THE LOCOMOTIVE CLUB OF GREAT BRITAIN

THE DORSET BELLE RAIL TOUR

Sunday 27th. February 1966

Map of route

LEGEND.
ROUTE OF TOUR
CLOSED STATIONS
OTHER LINES
LINES LIFTED

The usual detailed plan produced for the LCGB to accompany the tour literary. This was part of an A5 brochure so apologies for the folds. (We did not think Les would appreciate having it ironed!)

This Junction was remotely controlled from Brookwood and here we took the 'new' 1870 cut-off; previously, Farnham and Alton having been served via Guildford.

We were scheduled to stop at Alton 'for working purposes', presumably to take the single line tablet, but in the event crept through on schedule at 10.05am meaning *Clan Line* had a run at Medstead Bank. We had been given thirteen minutes to reach the summit but with the regulator wide open *Clan Line* raised her skirts and veritably stormed up to Medstead in ten minutes. This ultimately resulted in our having to wait subsequently at Alresford home signal for nine minutes to enable the scheduled 9.53am Southampton Central – Alton, a two car 'Hampshire' DMU, to cross; fortunately the diesel was running to time.

After a delay at Winchester Junction, presumably to allow a train on the down main line to take precedence, we followed and eventually sailed into Southampton six minutes late. Six minutes were allowed here for water and we saved just one leaving at 11.11am, five minutes down.

Despite a leisurely forty-five minutes having been set for the 29 miles to Bournemouth, we continued a gentle cruise, threading our way through Bournemouth Central at 11.58am, eight minutes late. It didn't get any better; we arrived at Wareham at 12.27pm still seven minutes down.

Here, two sister engines, ex-LMS Ivatt Class 2 2-6-2Ts Nos 41284 and 40301, both Weymouth (70G) locomotives, awaited on the 'Up' line, with safety valves blowing furiously.

After *Clan Line* had taken refuge in the 'Down' Swanage Bay our companions for the next stages of the journey ran forward, bunker first, to take charge. Fortunately by now it had also become a bright late winter's day in Dorset.

The pair took us forward, turning off at Worgret Junction to Swanage where we stopped at the Home Signal to allow the lead engine, No 41301, to run forward into the Goods Yard loop, opposite the then disused locomotive shed, whilst the train engine No 41284 took the train into the station. This was to overcome the problem that the head shunt in the station permitted entry for only one locomotive. Then 41301 rejoined the train at its head, both also still showing they had plenty of steam to spare.

Travelling back 'Up' the branch there was a photographic stop at Corfe Castle. At that period Corfe Castle station exuded a very woebegone air, despite the fact that it remained the only passing loop on the branch.

Given that the Swanage Railway's subsequent prosperity is now common knowledge, it is difficult to believe the importance that Corfe Castle Station has since taken on. The rejuvenated Swanage Railway ran its first diesel-powered passenger train back into Wareham Station on 13 June 2017. This was followed on 26 May the following year when a new partnership emerged with the then operator SouthWest Trains running the first regular timetabled service since 1969 from Corfe Castle directly to Waterloo on Summer Saturdays and indeed to other parts of their network.

Arrival at Wareham with the two tank engines ready to attach to the train as soon as No 35028 is clear.

Shunting move at Swanage. This was necessary as the engine release crossover at the far end of the platform could not accommodate the pair of engines together. Note also the train is longer than the platform.

Photo stop at Corfe Castle, and dare we say a seemingly disinterested looking driver on No 41284.

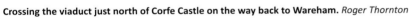

Crossing the viaduct just north of Corfe Castle on the way back to Wareham. *Roger Thornton*

Following the return to Wareham, No 35028 was reattached and is seen here heading west towards Dorchester and Weymouth. *Roger Thornton*

Returning to 1966, by the time we arrived back at Wareham we were still five minutes down on schedule. *Clan Line* had been waiting patiently for us in the Down Bay so on our arrival it was a simple task of running her forward to take up her position at the head of the train and we were able to leave on schedule at 1.46pm.

There followed a very smooth run on to Weymouth, arriving on time at 2.14pm. We were followed down by the two Ivatt Tanks but both had to go on shed to take water. Meanwhile another Ivatt Class 2MT 2-6-2T No 41298, the station pilot, ran forward to take the empty stock of our train out of the platform in order to release *Clan Line* for it to go to shed for servicing.

Of course this took time and although thirty-one minutes had been allowed for the operations, we nevertheless left Weymouth six minutes late at 2.51pm. The pair of Ivatts made a valiant, terrier-like, assault on the 1 in 50 climb from the still extant Radipole Halt, to Bincombe Tunnel. Still climbing we passed Dorchester Junction seven minutes late but with the aid of some recovery time set into the timetable we arrived at Maiden Newton having pulled back a minute and a half on schedule.

In 1965, almost contemporaneously with the demise of steam, the goods service was withdrawn from the Bridport line. This resulted in the branch effectively becoming little more than a nine-mile long siding. It was this that accounted for the next set of locomotive manoeuvres. No 41301 moved off the head to run around the train and take up its position at the rear so we became 'topped and tailed' for our run down to Bridport. This manoeuvre extended our late running to fourteen minutes.

The Bridport branch also ran through some difficult terrain. After initially falling on a gradient of 1 in 100, we entered the valley of the little River Hooke and followed it up towards its source near Toller – the former name of the river – climbing the four miles at 1 in 150/200. Just beyond Toller, after a small climb at 1 in 85 across moorland, the rest of the journey was downhill all the way this time through the valley of the River Asker.

About a mile and a half outside Bridport was Bradpole Level Crossing, over what was then a relatively minor road and operated by train crew as and when a train passed. After a leisurely run we stood at Bridport so photographs could be taken, of what was probably the last steam train ever to visit the town.

The pair of tank engines being serviced at Weymouth and made ready for the hard work ahead.

No 41301 leading as the pair tackle the stiff climb through Upwey on their way to Maiden Newton. At this stage seemingly with some steam to spare.

Roger Thornton

End of the line at Bridport – although years before the branch had continued on to West Bay. Neither crew not participants could have imagined the difficulties that lay ahead for the return journey.

Leaving at 4.26pm we were still eleven minutes late by schedule. All went well until the stop at Bradpole. Here from the necessary standing start the pair of Ivatts put in a courageous effort, attacking the initial 1 in 62 climb followed by a further mile and a half at 1 in 52. We staggered through Powerstock at walking pace. The Ivatts were struggling and shortly after this they stalled. Perplexed passengers were glued to windows. After an extended interlude allowing the two tank engines to catch their breath they were coaxed into a final assault and we sallied forth wheezing over the summit at Toller.

The net result was we arrived back at Maiden Newton thirty-five minutes down and it took all of the time allocated for the two engines to resume their duties in double-headed formation. However, there was still plenty of work for the pair, and further climbing to be done.

Maiden Newton is set at 328 feet above sea level and Evershot, the second highest village in the county, is the summit of the climb from Weymouth. Here the Dorset downland rises to 574 feet. So henceforth the Ivatts again set about their task. Seventeen minutes had been allowed for the

thirteen miles to Yeovil Pen Mill but despite their best efforts it took us all of twenty minutes to accomplish it.

Amid the gathering gloom at Pen Mill, the two locomotives had to run around the train yet again before we left at 5.57pm for Yeovil Junction. The traditional route between these two stations had been via Yeovil Town although the two routes, ex-GWR and Southern, did run parallel to one another. On 13 October 1943, in the middle of WW2, a connection was made between the two for the first time so enabling trains to run direct between Pen Mill and the Junction. It was this chord we now traversed to get there.

At Yeovil Junction, original 'Battle of Britain' Pacific No 34057 *Biggin Hill*, then a Salisbury (70E) based engine, awaited us. With some smart station work we were away at 6.10pm; now twenty-two minutes late. The Itinerary told us, "*From Yeovil Junction to Waterloo the main interest will be in the locomotive performance, especially in view of the uncertainty of future steam workings between Yeovil and Salisbury.*"

In this respect *Biggin Hill* did reasonably well, running the thirty-nine miles to Salisbury in a respectable fifty minutes;

In the gathering gloom of the late winter afternoon at Yeovil Pen Mill. Next the train will make its way to Yeovil Junction for the final leg back to Waterloo.

fine but hardly exhilarating. After taking water, in half the time scheduled, we ran through Worting Junction still twenty-two minutes late. From here-on, having also now lost our path, we obviously ran into traffic. Gradually we fell further and further behind until our final arrival at Waterloo at 8.49pm was thirty-four minutes late.

For many of the participants this must have been a disappointment but for me it was probably one of the more interesting railtours I ever experienced.

With hindsight perhaps too much had been expected of the tank engines on the severe gradient. Consequently, after the train stopped for the crew to open and close the gates at Bradpole Crossing, and from a standing start with one engine either end of the train, there was little opportunity for a co-ordinated attack on Toller bank. However this locomotive formation was inevitable with no run round facilities available at Bridport, since the branch was now single line throughout.

The Bridport branch staggered on until eventual closure on 5 May 1975 and coincidentally was one of the last closures directly connected with the Beeching Report. The site of the former Bridport Station is now smothered by a Morrisons supermarket and the town is better known amongst 'Real Ale' drinkers as the home of 'Palmer's Ales', an independent brewery still in family hands at a time when many such brewers have been absorbed into larger combines.

It is now difficult to believe more than fifty years have elapsed. However there is much to reflect on; the Swanage Railway has experienced a wonderful renaissance. The chord from Pen Mill to Yeovil Junction still appears to be extant, witness its use by South West Trains in the summer of 2017 when in conjunction with the Swanage Railway it ran a Saturday through train from Salisbury via Yeovil, Weymouth (reverse) and Wareham (reverse) to Corfe Castle. The Yeovil chord is specifically retained for use when required as a connecting diversion between the former GWR and SR routes, cementing the reason for its construction, during the war years.

Indeed, apart from the section of line between Alresford and Winchester Junction section and of course the Bridport Branch, the rest of the route may still be traversed by train today.

Full Contents List for *Southern Way*

'Preview' through to Issue No 49

We have often been asked is there a list of contents for the Southern Way? A short answer is 'yes' – but also 'no'. The reason for this being that several excellent lists appear on the internet compiled by private individuals but up to now we have not included a list of retrospective contents rather than a full index. With this No 50 issue we are delighted to put right that omission.

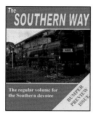
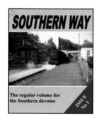
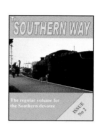
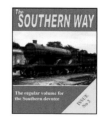

Issue 4
September 2008

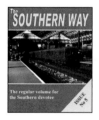

Issue 5
January 2009

Issue 6
April 2009

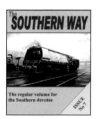

Issue 7
July 2009

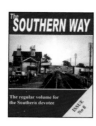
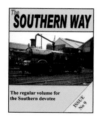

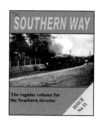
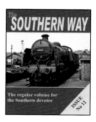

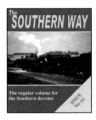
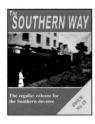

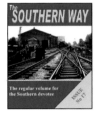

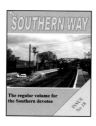
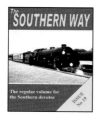
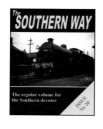
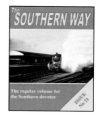
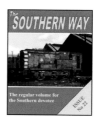

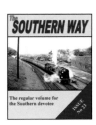
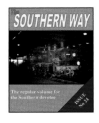
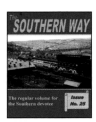
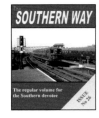
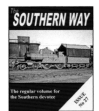

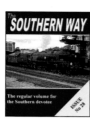
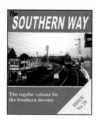
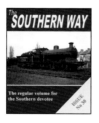
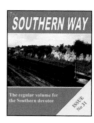
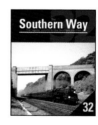

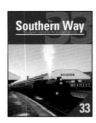
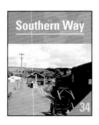
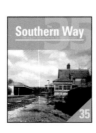
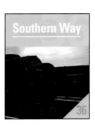

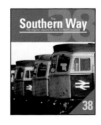

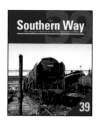
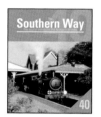
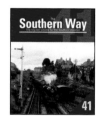
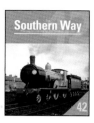

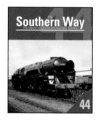

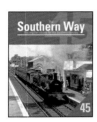
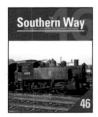
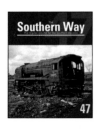

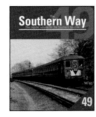